TABLE OF CONTENTS

Page

CHAPTER 1

INTRODUCTION

In 610, a little known merchant in a town in the center of the Arabian Peninsula called Mecca brought a new religion to the world. Mohammed brought the people of the Middle East a religion that would unite and motivate them to conquer all of North Africa, Persia, and much of Eastern Europe. Several Islamic cultures would participate in that conquest creating huge empires called caliphates. These caliphates would move several times from the death of Mohammed until the demise of the final Islamic empire in 1918.

The Muslims ruled much of the known world from Persia to Spain for centuries. Mohammed and the Arabs created the first caliphate by attacking and conquering their neighbors in Persia and then the Byzantine Empire. The next rulers, the Mamluks, fought the Crusaders and defeated the Mongols thus preventing the Middle Eastern world from falling into either permanent Christian or Mongol rule. After defeating the Mamluks, the Ottoman Turks consolidated power and completed the collapse of the Byzantines. The Ottomans followed with an invasion of Europe that ended at the gates of Vienna. While all of these conquests are notable, the fact remains that none of the Islamic empires remain in power today. The main reason for the fall of the last Islamic empire was the failure of their army to adapt to modern technology, concepts, and tactics. Today, modern Islamic armies continue to be inferior in their use of technology, concepts, and tactics.

Problem Statement

The challenges of Islamic armies of the past are now the challenges of any modern Islamic nation attempting to modernize its army. There is a distinct pattern within Islamic military history from the time before the introduction of Islam to the present. A distinct "Islamic Way of War" exists throughout the history of Islam. One component of this way of war is how Islamic armies adapt to material and conceptual change. This "Islamic Way of War" begins with the Parthians in 238 BC and continues through the armies of Islamic empires and nation states and includes a set of characteristics that are not conducive to modernizing. When any nation attempts to help a modern Islamic army, that nation must be cognizant of these unchangeable characteristics seen clearly over the entirety of Islamic history.

Thesis

Islamic armies possess an ability to assimilate technology, concepts, and tactics from external sources, but refuse to assimilate the associated culture of that technology. Instead, they choose to use foreign ideas and technology in a distinctly Islamic manner. Likewise, the Islamic nations do not display an ability to create original technology from within. This inability to utilize the imported technology, concepts, and tactics effectively inevitably adversely affects the performance of Islamic armies.

This thesis investigates the use of technology, concepts, and tactics from the pre-Mohammed Persians, through the rise of Mohammed and the Arabs into the "Golden Age of Islam," the Seljuk Turks, the Mamluks, and finally to the Ottomans. It examines the fighting technology, concepts, and tactics of each empire separately in light of the external threat to their empire. Research addresses both the land and sea components of

2

the Islamic war efforts while focusing where the Islamic empires focused, land operations. Its main focus is on the rise of the Islamic armies and the inability of the Mamluks, and later the Ottomans, to change in light of the threat to their empires. Clearly, the importance of this thesis can be seen in current efforts to modernize not only the Iraqi and Afghan Army and Police, but also in the ongoing reform of the Egyptian, Jordanian, Lebanese, and Saudi militaries. It is only through these allies that the United States can create and then maintain peace in that region.

Definitions

The most important definition in this thesis is that of technology, concepts, and tactics. This term relates to any material invention, idea, or tactical/operational solution that the Islamic armies took from another nation and inculcated into their fighting method. These include but are not limited to spears, bows, armor, saddles, stirrups, siege methods and equipment, large and small firearms, naval technology, and the rise of the professional soldier and army. This thesis does not continue into the modern Islamic army period and therefore weapons of World War I and later are not included.

The term "Islamic Army" in this thesis refers to armies of selected Islamic empires. These include the armies of the pre-Mohammedan Parthian and Sassanid Persian Empires, Mohammed and the Companions, the Caliphates of the Ummayids and the Abbasids, the Seljuk Turks, the Mamluks of Egypt, and finally the Ottoman Empire. The time period of this thesis begins with the rise of the Parthians in 238 BC to the fall of the Ottoman Empire at the end of World War I in 1918.

Limitations

The primary limitation for this thesis is the lack of primary source information in several periods. This limitation begins with the Parthian and Sassanid Persians and extends through the Ottomans. The number and quantity of primary sources are greater during victories while much less for defeats. For example, the Battle of Lepanto during the Ottoman period has several primary sources from the West, but less than five primary sources from the Ottomans. Many of the sources are poorly detailed. This is especially true of sources on the Parthian and Sassanid Persians.

Another limitation is translation. Many primary sources are in Ancient Persian, several dialects of Arabic, and Turkish. This thesis was written from the translations of several documents from their original language into another and finally into English.

The existing data has been filtered several times and in many cases censored by the ruler of the time. In several cases, Caliphs and Sultans threatened or executed writers of controversy. This affects the writing of source material and thus of this thesis.

Assumptions

This thesis assumes cultural characteristics of the Middle East are common in all the armies of the region in the period studied. Those characteristics are also included in the Islamic religion as practiced in the Middle East during the period.

Literature Review

The literature regarding Islam is immense. Further, the literature regarding each culture is equally large. Together, the literature is nearly overwhelming. Modern warfare in the Middle East between Europeans, Israelis, and Islamic nations has generated even more. These sources are primarily books using primary and secondary sources. Each of

them views a specific culture and in most cases examines military qualities in some

detail. Some texts combined the cultures over time to produce an examination of Islamic

military history from beginning to end. However, no sources examined the pre-Islamic

armies of the region to use as a comparison.

<u>The Parthian and Sassanid Persians</u>

The pre-Islamic period of the Parthian and Sassanid Persians is limited in primary

sources; however, Xenophon's *Anabasis: The March Up Country* provided primary

source information about the methodology of the pre-Parthian civilization in the Middle

East and of the Greeks that they fought. Kaveh Farrokh's *Shadows in the Desert*

provided a detailed examination of the Parthians as well as a detailed description of the

Battle of Gaugamela. Victor Davis Hanson's *Carnage and Culture* also provided a

detailed description of the Battle of Gaugamela as well as why Darius and his army

performed so poorly. Peter Wilcox's *Rome's Enemies (3): Parthians and Sassanid*

Persians gives a side-by-side description of the technology, concepts, and tactics that

proved invaluable to the writing of this thesis. The description of *catapharacts* and

clibarnius as well as the —Parthian Shot" enabled a visualization of a battlefield during

the Parthian and Sassanid period.

In conjunction with Farrokh's work, Louis Dimarco's *War Horse: A History of*

the Military Horse and Rider provided a wealth of information on the Battle of Carrahae

that demonstrated the Persian ability to defeat an infantry-based army, in this case the

Romans, with their cavalry. Michael Dodgeon and Samual Lieu's *The Roman Eastern*

Frontier and the Persian Wars (AD 226-363) contained a series of primary sources that

detailed the Battle of Carrahae and others in small, paragraph-sized works.

The Early Islamic Armies – 600-1500 AD

The Early Islamic period's extended time frame dictated a need for sources for

specific periods internal to the larger period and references for the overall period from the

beginning of Islam to the end of the Ottoman Empire. Sir John Glubb's *A Short History*

of the Arab Peoples as well as Oliver Spaulding and Hoffman Nickerson's *Ancient and*

Medieval Warfare, George Nafzinger and Mark Walton's *Islam at War: A History*, Amir

Siqqidi's *Decisive Battles of Islam*, Phillip K. Hitti's *The Arabs: A Short History*, and

Hugh Kennedy's *Great Arab Conquests: How the Spread of Islam Changed the World*

We Live In provided these sources. All of these deliver detailed timelines in narrative

form that enabled a linear examination of the history of Islam. Inside of these texts are

quotes from the Koran that elaborate on specific aspects of this thesis.

The Greek chronicle of Theophanes and the Arabic chronicle of Ibn al-Athir

supply primary sources for the Battle of Poitiers. Hanson's *Carnage and Culture* serves

as the best secondary source for that battle as it provides information from other primary

sources as well as analysis and a wealth of secondary sources in its bibliography.

The Battle of Manzikert is described in Brian T. Carey's ―Debacle at Manzikert,

1071: A Prelude to the Crusades" from *Medieval History* as well as the primary sources

in De Expugatione Terrae Sanctae per Saladinum, [The Capture of the Holy Land by

Saladin], ed. Joseph Stevenson. Another secondary source for this battle this is

extremely useful is William J. Hamblin, ―Saladin and Muslim Military Theory" from

Military History, for its description of the theory behind the attacking Islamic army.

The greatest resource for study of the Mamluk period is James Waterson's *The Knights of Islam: The Wars of the Mamluks*. This book, while a secondary source, delivers a detailed history of the Mamluks from their beginnings as slaves to their decline under the Ottomans and then their appointment as governors of Baghdad. It is an indispensable book for this period. Paul E. Chevedden's ―Black Camels and Blazing Bolts: The Bolt-Projecting Trebuchet in the Mamluk Army" in *Mamluk Studies Review* along with David Ayalon's *Gunpowder and Firearms in the Mamluk Kingdom: A Challenge to a Mediaeval Society* add to the specific weapon system knowledge of the section on the Mamluks.

The Rise and Fall of the Ottomans

The basis for this chapter comes from Peter Sugar's *Southeastern Europe Under Ottoman Rule, 1354-1804*. This short description of the Ottoman Empire enables the reader to understand the internal dynamics of the court and the military. Nafzinger and Walton's *Islam at War* remains an important text for a view of the Ottoman navy and the Janissaries. Andrew Wheatcroft's *The Ottomans: Mirroring Images* established a base for the competency and motivation of the Ottoman soldier while *The Early and Modern Ottomans: Remapping the Empire* by Virginia H. Aksan and Daniel Goffman, Ed. provided additional information on the Ottoman sailor. In addition to the texts referenced in the literature review of the early Islamic armies, Bernard Lewis's *The Middle East*, Max Boot's *War Made New: Weapons, Warriors, and the Making of the Modern World*, and Christian Archer's *World History of Warfare* filled in the gaps of detail in time periods covered.

Methodology

The methodology used to examine Islamic armies through time is linear. This thesis begins with the early empires in the Middle East and continues to the near present. It ends with an analysis of why Islamic armies are not able to capitalize on technology, concepts, and tactics.

Each chapter begins with a general history of the period followed by specific battles or events in the period that highlight the Islamic army's failure to adapt. Chapter 2 focuses on the Parthian and Sassanid Persians and examines their fighting methods and technology. Chapter 3 examines the pre-Modern Islamic armies of Mohammed to the Mamluks. Chapter 4 focuses exclusively on the Ottoman Empire, its rise to power, and steady decline over four hundred years. This leads to a conclusion in chapter 5, where this thesis presents a consideration of modern Islamic armies over several wars, reasons for why Islamic armies fail to adapt, and recommendations for those who wish to change an Islamic army.

Summary

The significance of this study is its use by those who commit to the modernization of an Islamic army. This thesis focuses on the cultural background of the Islamic armies of the past as well as methods for change that were successful. Its significance goes beyond highlighting specific failures, but to show that after a thousand years or more of successful warfighting an inability to accept technology, concepts, and tactics occurred. The U.S. military, in conjunction with NATO and others, are currently attempting to assist the modernization of several Islamic armies simultaneous with the approval of their leaders. This task is great and requires a sensitivity toward, and awareness of, the history

of Islamic armies and innovation.

CHAPTER 2

THE PARTHIAN AND SASSANID PERSIANS

There were several important cultures in the Middle East before the rise of Islam: Egyptians, Phoenicians, and Persians being among the best known. This thesis will focus on the pre-Islamic empires of the Parthian and the Sassanid Persians as the Egyptians and Phoenicians fought in the ancient period. While it may seem obvious that a paper on any Islamic way of war should start with the Prophet Mohammed, this paper will use cultures and empires before Mohammed to demonstrate a baseline of ability in some cultures or inability in others to use technology to its fullest.

The period of Persian history that this chapter will examine begins before the Parthians by examining Artaxerxes and the Achaemenids. Warriors in these battles fought as individuals rather than armies and thus these battles should be considered ancient warfare rather than pre-modern warfare. For example, Artaxerxes and Cyrus personally fought each other with Cyrus delivering the fatal blow.[1] The next critical event during this time was the invasion of the Greeks described by the *Anabasis*, however the army that fought the Greeks was not wholly Persian but a conglomerate of cultures. The final pre-Parthian period of combat involved the Greek heavy infantry of Alexander and its phalanx against the people of Persia and the surrounding area. While the people of Persia had been able to develop their cavalry techniques, they had not developed their combined arms tactics--cavalry and infantry performing together--well enough to resist the combined arms warfare of Alexander.[2] Their core competencies were overwhelmed by Alexander's system. The pre-Selucid people of Iran fought with ancient methods that did not constitute an army and the Selucids were simply a Greek hold-over army,

therefore, to examine this period, this thesis must begin with the Parthians.

Technology of the Parthians

From the outset, the Parthian change in combat methods came in the form of new

technology, new doctrine, and organization. While there was change, it did not reflect

Roman or Western influence. Instead, change reflected the ideas of the Persians: shock

action from horseback combined with harassing archery to enable the cavalry. The ideas

and formation of the Parthian army were based on Darius' Persian army that was defeated

by Alexander at Gaugamela. The cavalry of Darius's army was mainly heavy cavalry

with chariots, elephants, and archers in support. Darius fought with a method that he had

used many times before; he placed his best infantry in the center with his cavalry on the

flanks as the Persian army was much larger than the Macedonian and thus could easily

attack their flanks. Chariots would ride forward and into the Macedonian infantry lines.

Archers would remain stationary to fire at the Macedonians as they attacked.

To defeat Darius at Gaugamela, Alexander neutralized the effects of the chariots'

charge by having his infantry link shields thus the chariots rode over them in many

places. Alexander also created intentional gaps in the paths of the chariots which

canalized them into his infantry formations and enabled his infantry to attack them as

they passed.[3] Alexander used his cavalry to counter the flanking movements by placing a

detachment on the left to delay Darius' cavalry and personally leading a detachment on

the right. As the right flank under Alexander made contact with Darius cavalry,

Alexander and his formation turned back toward the center of Darius formation and

attacked. Darius' left flank cavalry could not respond nor could they attack Alexander's rear as Alexander had brought up pelasts and archers with the cavalry that fixed Darius cavalry.[4] Alexander then countercharged into Darius' center and destroyed it. Darius fled the field and the battle turned into a rout. While the courage and brilliance of Alexander enabled the Macedonians to win, Darius' failure to enable his cavalry with mobile missileers also contributed to his defeat. Clearly the army of the Parthians needed something to counter this. They needed a horse-mounted archer.

The Parthian Heavy Cavalryman

After the death of Alexander, the Macedonian empire split into four smaller empires. The Parthians found themselves fighting the Seleucids, a smaller copy of Alexander's army. The Parthians learned from their mistakes in their dealings with Alexander and the Seleucids and used a number of technologies, bows and armor foremost among them, and the associated concepts and tactics to their advantage. These adaptations to the threat included the ability to conduct cavalry charges into infantry lines as the Macedonians had done and having an archer who was able to move and support the cavalry. The adaptations enabled the Parthians to conduct shock attacks and then press the battle toward the complete destruction of the enemy in a manner not previously possible.

The establishment of a new army changed the Persian fighting method as the Parthians created a combined arms army much like Alexander's. They based this army on heavy cavalry, called cataphracts or *clibarnii*, with mounted archers in support unless the terrain dictated otherwise.[5] It was cavalry-based because the Parthians, unlike the Greeks, thought of infantry as a lowly pursuit and cavalry for those of noble birth.[6] The heavy cavalry featured heavily armored horsemen with two-handed lances which did not allow them to carry shields. The horses also carried heavy armor to defeat the infantry slashing attacks of the enemy. To better facilitate the horseman in the saddle, the Parthians changed their saddle from an Achaemenid —carpet saddle" to a more advanced saddle which was curved at the front and back.[7] This saddle gave the Parthian lancer the ability to better hold on while charging and provided a steadier platform for the Parthian archer while riding. While there were saddles, they were not in abundance and were very primitive. Most Parthian heavy cavalrymen, called cataphracts, simply held on with the strength of their thighs.[8]

The Horse Archer

The heavy cavalryman was the center of the formation in the Parthian army, but it was the Parthian horse archer that many times either won the battle or at least enabled the Parthian lancer to defeat a demoralized enemy. This is easily seen at the Battle of Carrhae when archers charged and fired until the Romans were unable to mount any resistance.[9] The introduction of a much improved saddle allowed the Parthian horse archer to fire from a stable platform with much less fear of falling off the horse. In fact, it enabled the famed —Parthian shot."[10]

The Parthian archer was lightly armored. More often than not, he was unarmored because mobility was his best defense against the Seleucid or Roman infantry that had not adopted archers to compliment their infantry-based formations. Primarily, the archer was used against other light cavalrymen in skirmishes on the plains. His duty was participating in raiding, harassment, and pursuit, but when organized with the heavy cavalry, he would fire from horseback in support of the cavalry charge.[11] This important difference enabled the archer to be mobile during the battle and ensured that the cavalry would have support throughout the battle. He sometimes carried a sword or other bladed weapon, but it was for defense only. His purpose was to prepare the enemy's line for assault by the heavy cavalry. His primary weapon was a composite bow made of sinew, wood, and bone; powerful enough to penetrate the armor of the steppes and even the armor of the Romans. His strength lay in the number of arrows that he could carry and then fire. In the earlier years, it was simple to produce the number of arrows that would be needed for a raiding party or a brief attack. To produce the number of arrows required both tactically in battle and strategically in the defense of an empire would require a new way of thinking.[12]

Parthian Doctrine to Best Utilize their Technology

Two different sets of circumstances brought the Parthians to power, and then kept them in it. First, the rise of the Parthians was not due to some advantage over the Seleucids, but internal strife among the Seleucids.[13] Second, the army of Parthian King Merhdad I (123-88 BC) generally considered the ruler who consolidated Parthian power and destroyed the Seleucid Empire, was an effective fighting force but still not steeped in the tactics that would make it famous. The army was cavalry-based; infantry was an afterthought because they were too slow and not of noble birth. Speed was necessary because of the method of fighting. Arrows flew and charges followed or happened simultaneously. This led to a doctrine of preparation of the enemy's line with arrows and then a massed, armored cavalry attack into what was perceived as the enemy's softest point.[14]

It is unclear as to why the two types of cavalry developed independent of each other. What is clear is that the horse archers had come from raiding days, a Persian, and

14

especially Parthian, specialty. The heavy cavalry had it origins from the Scythians, from whom the Parthians are descended.[15] The Parthians that followed the Achaemenids designed their army to fight the infantry-based army of the Seleucids. The Parthians studied the defeat of Darius and created a force to counter the Seleucids. Clearly there was some innovation happening in the Parthian royalty and ranks.

In 53 BC, an army of five legions (approximately 28,000-40,000 foot soldiers accompanied by 400 cavalrymen) commanded by Marcus Licinius Crassus, a member of the Triumvirate and the Roman Governor of Syria, invaded Persia to destroy the Parthians. Crassus, ignoring all military advice, chose to cross the Euphrates and press the offensive. His legions came to the open desert of Carrhae. Unlike former battles, the Romans did not face an enemy organized to charge across the open field and into Roman lines as Darius had done to the Macedonians. That type of attack could have easily been defeated with caltrops in front to cut the feet of the horses and infantrymen and then a battle between the well-trained Roman legionnaires and the poorly trained Parthian infantry.[16] The crafty Parthian general, Surena, organized his army from the outset with mainly mounted archers and a small amount of heavy cavalry. This in effect defeated the Romans usual tactics and allowed the Parthians to defeat the Romans without closing to hand-to-hand range. The Parthians simply fired volleys of arrows, then went back to restock their quivers, and returned quickly for more slaughter.[17] The resupply came from a supply train that provided arrows from a Parthian arrow factory. It was the greatest Roman defeat since Cannae resulting in 20,000 Roman soldiers dead and another 20,000 in captivity.[18] The Parthians proved their expertise at applying military technology to defeat the Romans.[19]

The Parthians represent a clear change in the technology, the doctrine that supports that technology, and the logistical support for that technology. The Parthians adopted a cavalry-based army that did not fight like the Greeks. There was not what Victor Hanson would call —decisive combat.”[20] Not only did the Parthians adopt technologies that enabled them to contribute to the fall of the Seleucids, but they adopted technologies that enabled them to conduct their method of fighting and then defeat the forces of the mightiest empire on the planet at the time. While the Parthians did adopt technology, they used it to support their tactics. It was still a cavalry fight; there were no large stationary formations of bowmen as would be seen later in Europe. While the Parthians remained militarily strong, a dynastic struggle enabled the Sassanid Persians to consolidate power in their area until they were stronger than the Parthians. What remained of the Parthian Empire eventually became subordinate to the Sassanids.

Technology of the Sassanids

If the Parthians were able to bring about the unification of the Persian people, then the Sassanids truly advanced it. The first king of the Sassanid line, Ardashir I, declared himself king in 208 as the pendulum of military might in the area swung away from the Parthians to the Romans.[21] The Sassanid system of central government was much more effective than the Parthians. It allowed for a central financing of the empire and provided for industrial support.[22] It enabled them to defeat the Romans in several battles. These battles saw the empire of the Sassanids expand from a central Asian power to the ruler of most of the Middle East. Their hold on power spanned over 300 years.[23]

What the Parthians began in cavalry-based tactics, the Sassanids continued. The Sassanid armies drew directly from the doctrine and equipment of the Parthinans. In fact,

16

many of the minor Parthian nobles were allowed to continue to serve in the Sassanid

Empire. The nobility of the cavalry continued along with the professionalism of the

horse archers. The difference lay not in a revolution in military affairs, but the

progression of technology from Parthia to the Sassanids in a simple evolution in armor

and tactics.[24]

The Sassanid heavy cavalry became progressively heavier. Armor grew from

simple caps to full face masks in which only the eyes of the Sassanid cavalryman could

be seen.[25] The primary enemy of the Sassanids, the Roman Empire, increasingly

employed the one thing that they had not in prior engagements, archers. The Romans

primarily used mercenary horse and foot archers to soften the Sassanid cavalry prior to

the assault by Roman infantry and cavalry or prior to receiving the Sassanid attack. The

Romans had learned from Carrhae that their powerful legions needed a missile capability

and they simply bought it. The Romans were then able to inflict the same damage from

distance that previously only the Parthians could. The Sassanids had to react to the

changing battlefield and did it with armor.[26]

The armor went from the lighter ringed armor with a smaller amount of

reinforcing plates to a ringed mail with nearly all scale cover. Sassanid heavy cavalry

became super-heavy cavalry. This was a trend not only in the armor of the lancer, but

also that of the horse. Wilcox describes that ―the whole throng of horses was protected

by covering of leather."[27]

In order to defeat missile attacks from archers as well as slingers and javelin

throwers, the Sassanid archers also became more heavily armored. The archer looked

less and less like an archer capable of pursuit and more and more like an armored heavy

17

cavalryman. As both types of cavalry became heavier, the need for two separate formations became less. The history of Sassanid cavalry from the birth of the empire to its death at the hands of the Arabs is one of the multi-functional horseman. The lancer merged with the archer to create a cavalryman that could do both as well as fight dismounted if needed. This again shows the evolution of Sassanid tactics away from a Western, infantry-based method, but rather continuing defeat of the infantry with cavalry.[28]

The Sassanids did not change their weapons. There was very little change in the types of weapons the Sassanids carried from those of the Parthians. The bows, lances, and swords, when carried, were virtually unchanged revealing that the Sassanids viewed them as successful and therefore not in need of change.[29]

In addition to the changes in armor and organization, the Sassanids acquired siege technology from the Romans. During the reign of Shapur II (r 309-379), a great reformer of the Sassanid Empire, the Sassanid army besieged Nisiblis. Shapur split his army for a siege and after the city was surrounded, erected towers, and reduced the city by having his archers climb the towers and fire downward into the city while his forces simultaneously dug at the walls.[30]

During the Battle of Singara, the Sassanids not only used their significant archer ability to overwhelm the Romans, but they used captured Roman siege engines against them.[31] This was demonstrated by the Sassanid use of a Roman battering ram to batter a tower and open the city walls.[32] This is a far cry from the Parthians and shows an ability to take technology--siege engines--and the associated culture--conducting the siege of a city--and use it. The Sassanids used the siege technology to conduct a siege in the same manner as the Romans. It was not used as a means to soften the city with arrows or missile attacks; it was used to press decisive battle. Siege technology is not usually associated with Parthian cavalry-based warfare, but the Sassanids used it in conjunction with their existing method of warfare to continue the spread of empire.

The Sassanids also took from the Romans the concept of building walls. In the 7th century AD, the Arabs began their raiding and forceful occupation of Sassanid land in southern Persia. In order to create a buffer between them and the raiding Arabs, the Sassanid high command began to create a series of Romanesque walls on the border of what is now Iraq and Saudi Arabia. This technique clearly derived from the Roman's walls on the Syrian border became known as ―Khandaq-e-Shapur."[33]

While the changing of the army into a super-heavy cavalry based formation with archer capability, the siege capability, and the adoption of Roman defensive techniques are surely indicators that the Sassanids could change, it was not enough. Internal strife, Roman and later Byzantine attrition, and the Arab intrusions and later conquest caused the fall of the society.

Parthians and Sassanids Could Change

This chapter demonstrates that the pre-Islamic armies of the Persians, clearly the predecessors to the Islamic armies that would conquer in the coming centuries, could both adopt Western technology and use their own technology to its fullest to fight and defeat Western armies. The Parthian victory at Carrahae and the ability of the Sassanid Empire to resist of the Romans testify that they could confront the might of the Romans and change to meet their enemies' capabilities. In the span of 800 years from 138 BC-651 AD, the Parthians and Sassanids changed from the primitive cavalry and infantry armies of the Persians that fought the Greeks into a multi-purpose cavalry force that was capable of fighting from a distance or pressing an attack home while mounted or dismounted.[34]

What they refused to do was change their core competencies. It is clear that the Parthians and Sassanids kept their armies based in cavalry to maximize the life span of their nobility. Mobility was the key to the armies of both the Parthians and Sassanids. The use of archers to suppress or destroy an enemy's infantry or cavalry lines followed by a cavalry charge prevented the wholesale slaughter of a generation of Parthian nobility as was done in countless Greek battles. The culture needed to keep its nobility from dying en masse on the battlefield and thus kept them out of the thick of fighting unless absolutely needed. The Parthian and Sassanid methods of fighting were based on the manning of their formations; their cavalry became the best in the world while their infantry remained unchanged.

The Parthians and Sassanids both showed that their people could adopt technologies from their enemies. The Parthians adopted and adapted the arms and armor of their Seleucid neighbors to suit their own needs. The Sassanids refined the Parthian cavalry-based fighting method even further to combat the Romans while adopting siege techniques that enabled them to take their empire to the banks of the Mediterranean Sea. Both the Parthians and Sassanids reacted to capability gaps in technology by ignoring the emerging technology in favor of trying to make the old work against the new. While Darius III used chariots at Gaugamela with disastrous results, the Parthians and Sassanids gladly adopted new technologies to defeat their enemies. While both the Parthians and Sassanids adopted new technology, concepts, and tactics, they also took pre-existing technology and refined it, especially in the case of armor. Thus, they were able to make the older technology more effective. While the Parthians only capitalized on the previous technologies and developed doctrinal solutions to capability gaps in their use of cavalry against infantry, the Sassanids took siege technology from the Romans and made it their own. The end result of both cultures adoption of new technologies was an imperial army worthy of being called great.

---

[1] Xenophon, *The March up Country : a Translation of Xenophon's Anabasis*, trans. W.H.D Rouse (Ann Arbor: University of Michigan Press, 1964), 26-27.

[2] This is seen at the battle of Gaugamela. Farrokh describes the melee in *Shadows in the Desert*, 102-105, and Victor Davis Hanson, *Carnage and Culture* (New York: Anchor Books, 2001), 60-98. Both show the power of the organization of Alexander's army.

[3] Farrokh, Kaveh, *Shadows in the Desert* (Westminster, MD: Osprey Books, 2007),102-105. Farrokh describes Darius' desire to win as so great that he would even try an outdated weapon like the chariot. Hanson writes that when Alexander rode against the right flank and Darius charged with chariots, the ―Macedonians simply parted on cue for the scythed chariots and stabbed the drivers as they sped past. Darius' elephants apparently panicked or were let through the phalanx--or never made it to the front." Hanson, *Carnage and Culture*, 73.

[4] Hanson, *Carnage and Culture*, 67.

[5] The terms are used in almost all instances interchangeably. Wilcox says that the cataphracts were reasonably immune from hand-propelled missiles and arrows, less so from sling pellets or machine weapons. The most important fact about the cataphracts and the horse archers was that the Parthians did not arrange their army with a set number of either. They went to battle sometimes heavy on cataphracts and light on horse archers and other times heavy on archers and light on cataphracts depending on situation and terrain. Wilcox, *Rome's Enemies (3): Parthians and Sassanid Persians* (London: Osprey, 1986), 9.

[6] This is seen in the works of nearly every scholar of the Parthians and Sassanians, but especially in Farrokh, *Shadows in the Desert*, 131-135.

[7] Ibid., 132.

[8] See endnote 25 for more on cataphracts.

[9]Farrokh, *Shadows in the Desert*, 135.

[10]The "Parthian Shot" is called famous in most references and infamous in at least two, Farrokh's and Wilcox's. The Parthian Shot was a maneuver in which a group of horse archers would fire from the charge or stationary in a feint then turn and fire in the retrograde--not retirement or delay--thus being able to fire more arrows at infantry or cavalry in formation or in the pursuit of the feint. This softened the enemy infantry line for the assault of the Parthian heavy cavalry or lured the enemy cavalry into the Parthian cavalry in the case of a feint. The "Parthian Shot" is recognized today in the language of the pundits as the "parting shot."

[11]Farrokh calls this a "shock bowman." Farrokh, *Shadows in the Desert*, 133.

[12]At the battle or Carrhae, the Parthians were able to sustain their arrow attacks against the Romans by using a camel train. Each Parthian was able to fire his load of arrows and then turn away from the fight to re-stock and then rejoin the fray. This is said to have had a tremendous effect on the morale of the Romans at Carrhae who thought that they would be able to fight their preferred close battle once the Parthians ran out of arrows. Louis A. DiMarco, *War Horse: A History of the Military Horse and Rider* (Yardley, PA: Westholme Publishing, 2008), 71.

[13]Farrokh, *Shadows in the Desert*, 122.

[14]Farrokh calls this the "all-cavalry doctrine." He calls it a "clear division of labor between the lightly armored horse archers who _softened up' the enemy, and the heavily armored knights who then charged into the enemy with their lances." Ibid., 135.

[15]Ibid., 131.

[16]A caltrop is a spike made of nails or any other sharp material with a stable base that forms a tetrahedron. The spike is meant to point up to cut the feet of advancing infantrymen or the horses of the cavalry.

[17]This shows the value of the "camel train."

[18]There are conflicting numbers between sources. Regardless of the numbers, the Romans were badly defeated by the Parthians.

[19]Both Farrokh and Wilcox describe the battle in detail. Farrokh, *Shadows in the Desert*, 137-140, and Wilcox, *Rome's Enemies*, 16-22.

[20]Hanson, *Carnage and Culture*, 1-24.

[21]Farrokh, *Shadows in the Desert*, 178.

[22]Farokh also says that the Sassanids began interacting economically, artistically, and scientifically thus increasing trade through from the east. Ibid., 183.

[23]Wilcox says that while the Sassanian system began with a strong central government run by a Grand Vizier, near the end of the empire, the nobles of the Sassanian empire had near complete power to the point that the king was militarily and financially dependent on them. Wilcox, *Rome's Enemies*, 24.

[24]This is seen in the progression of heavy cavalry to "super-heavy cavalry" during the reign of Shapur II (r. 309-379). Farrokh, *Shadows in the Desert*, 200.

[25]These soldiers became known as catapharacts or clibarnius. According to Wilcox, Cataphract is derived from the Greek cataphractoi, meaning 'covered over.' The word clibarnius comes from one of the following: old Persian grivpan for 'warrior', Pahlavi grivpan for the pendant mail helmet defense, or from the Latin for a field oven, clibanus in a joking reference to the surely sweltering Persian soldiers inside the heavy armor. Wilcox, *Rome's Enemies*, 34. Both terms refer to "super-heavy" cavalrymen. It is best described by the writings of Ammianus Marcellinus, ". . . Moreover all the companies were clad in iron, and all parts of their bodies were covered with thick plates, so fitted that the stiff joints conformed with those of their limbs; and the forms of the human faces were so skillfully fitted to their head that, since their entire bodies were covered in metal, arrows that fell upon them could lodge only where they could see a little through tiny openings opposite the pupil of the eye, or where through the tips of their noses they were able to get a little breath." Michael H. Dodgeon, and Samuel N. C. Lieu, *The Roman Eastern Frontier and the Persian Wars (AD 226-363)* (London: Routledge, 2002), 190.

[26]This is a simple response to the Roman acquisition of archers. Wilcox, *Rome's Enemies*, 33.

[27]Ammianus Marcellinus, from Dodgeon and Lieu, *The Roman Eastern Frontier and the Persian Wars*, 190.

[28]Wilcox, *Rome's Enemies*, 33.

[29]The Sassanians had a very good record against the Romans as shown by Louis DiMarco. They were able to outlast them. DiMarco says that "its likely that they Roman cavalry simply were not equal to the Sassanians, and once the Roman cavalry were defeated, the Sassanians would have been able to wear down the Roman infantry in the great open spaces of the eastern frontier." DiMarco, *War Horse*, 73.

[30]Theodoret tells that Shapur II "divided his army as for a siege and completely surrounded the city, setting up machines for war, commissioning towers, erecting palisades, the areas between strewn with branches placed crosswise, then he ordered his troops to raise embankments and build towers against the city towers." Theodoret, Historia religiosa I, 11-12, ed. Canivet and Leroy-Molinghen, from Dodgeon and Lieu, *The Roman Eastern Frontier and the Persian Wars*, 184.

[31]Ammianus Marcellinus says "the cloud of arrows obscured the air, and the vast engines, of which the Persians had got possession of when they took Singara, scattered wounds everywhere." XIX, 2, 8, Ibid., 190.

[32]Ammianus Marcellinus says, "one day on the approach of evening a very heavy battering-ram was brought forward among other engines, which battered a round tower with repeated blows, at a point where we mentioned that the city had been laid open in a former siege." Ibid.

[33]This is literally translated as Shapur's Ditch as Shapur II was the current monarch. Shapur's ditch refers only to the Arabian facing walls. These walls were constructed to contain prevent Bedouin raids from the west. The walls were based on the Roman walls along the Roman-Syrian borders even further west. Farrokh, *Shadows in the Desert*, 199.

[34]These dates coincide with the ascent of Merhdad I, the first ruler of the Parthians, in 138 BC and the death of Yazdegird, the last ruler of the Sassanids, in 651 AD.

CHAPTER 3

THE EARLY ISLAMIC ARMIES – 600-1500 AD

In the early years of Islam, like European medieval military forces, armies looked

like armed mobs. Individual combat came first, and then group battle began. The armies

of the Caliph would fight their first two decades through the ―Great Conquests‖ in that

manner. In later periods, the Islamic people became the holders of the world‗s

knowledge and technology was included in that knowledge. Baghdad under the Abbasids

was the hub of knowledge in the world. During this period, Islamic armies imported

several technological advancements in this period: the stirrup, an improved bow, the

crossbow, siege engines, and finally cannon, and hand firearms. This chapter focuses on

Islamic armies of the ―Great Conquests‖ period of Islam, the Ummayid Empire, the

Abbasid Empire, the Seljuq Turks, and the Mamluks. An examination of select battles

shows that the armies of Islam in this period adopted the weapons and technology of

other people, without adopting any of the related cultural characteristics.

General Islamic History 600-1500 AD

Islam began in the 6th century based on the teachings of the Prophet Mohammed.

Mohammed remained the leader of the faithful until his death in 629. Upon his death,

three men served as ―caliph‖ or ―leader of the faithful:‖ Abu Bakr (r 632-634), Omar (r

634-644), and Uthman (r 644-656). At the death of Uthman, the last remaining

companion of the Prophet, there was a power struggle between the cousin and son-in-law

of the Prophet, Ali ibn abi Talib (598 or 600 – 661), and the greatest governor in the

Muslim nation, Muawiyah (r as Caliph 661 – 680), son of the Prophet‗s greatest Meccan opponent Abu Sufian (or Aby Sufiyan). Ali and Muawiyah battled several times until Ali

was assassinated by a Kharjite at his mosque in Kufa in 661.[1] Ali's son Hasan (625-670)

either willingly or under threat of force gave up his claim to the throne and Hasan's

brother, Husayn (626-680), claimed it as the grandson of the Prophet. Upon the death of

Ali in 661, Muawiyah likewise claimed the title of Caliph.[2] The mantle of Muslim

leadership transferred several times over the next 800 years. The Ummayids ruled from

661 until replaced by the house of Abbas--the Abbasid empire--in 750. The Seljuqs

followed the Abbasids from 967 until 1258 when they were defeated by the Mongols.

The Mamluks, former slaves to the Abbasids, defeated the Mongols at Ain Jaloot in

1260, and then prevented them from returning to the Middle East. They also prevented

Timur the Lame from plundering the region. The Mamluks were subsequently defeated

by the Ottoman Turks in battle near Cairo in 1517 and the Ottomans assumed the

caliphate until the modern era.

The Great Conquests – 600-658 AD

The age of the ―Great Conquests‖ is best summed up by Spaulding and

Nickerson:

> The Mohammedans, being originally desert men, preferred fighting on horseback.
> It had been their custom to skirmish but they now learned to charge home with the
> same extraordinary fanaticism which, in modern times, has made them such
> formidable foes in the Soudan and Afghanistan. In the apostolic age of
> Mohammedanism its warriors fought with the deliberate intention of seeking
> death. It was this spirit, and not the shortcomings of the forces opposed to them,
> which gave them their unbroken series of victories. It is hard enough to oppose
> such men with modern high-power weapons.[3]

The Muslims conquered all of the Near East, north to the Taurus Mountains, and

west to Tripoli in the nine years after the death of Mohammed.[4] The Muslim army also defeated the Byzantines, the power successor to the Roman Empire. They accomplished this against enemies with the technological advantage of archers while they attacked only with horse and steel.

Conflict is integral to early Islamic history. The empire began at Medina and then spread to Mecca. The Caliphs expanded the empire after the death of the Prophet into modern Iraq which contributed to the downfall of Persian Empire, and into modern Syria. By 638, the Caliphate ruled the Arabian Peninsula, Mesopotamia, and the area known as Syria. The threats to the Muslim empire were the Byzantine Empire which bordered to the north in Asia Minor, the west in Egypt, and the Mediterranean coast (modern Lebabon).

Arab and Islamic military forces in this period bore little resemblance to an organized army.[5] Islamic armies were little more than horse mounted, un-armored mobs. Through the early days of Islam, including the battles of Mecca (630) and the Qadisiya campaign (634-637), battle began with individual combat between champions. At the conclusion of individual combat, the armies engaged in a general melee of horse mounted raiders and infantrymen.[6] The commander of the Iraqi campaign of 624 was killed while personally trying to attack an elephant.[7] The average Islamic fighter, either *muhajirin* (the initial followers of Muhammed from Mecca) or *ansar* (literally supporters who were from Medina and the surrounding area), traveled light and fought on horseback or foot.[8]

The Islamic armies that campaigned from Mecca under the caliphates of Abu Bakr and Umar used little technology or tactics from either Western or Eastern influences. These armies fought much in the manner of the armies of the Prophet. It was not until the reforms of Sa'ad ibn abi Waqqas in 635 that the armies of Islam truly became organized armies.[9] Sa'ad organized them for battle in what he called divisions, yet they fought with the same weapons as the Persians. They used little armor and fought from camel or horseback as they had done before the conversion to Islam. The first appearance of new technology, concepts, and tactics came in the Qadisiyah Campaign in the Spring of 637 when the army of Sa'ad faced elephants for the first time in what would turn out to be the decisive battle of the Persian-Muslim conflict. The *catapharact* heavy cavalry described in chapter 2 still reigned supreme in Persia in the dying days of the Sassanid Empire. This cavalry was augmented with elephants. The four days of the battle began with individual combat as in all of the previous battles. During individual combat, the army of Islam was victorious by using a technology recently adapted from the Persian armies--the spear. The spear was the same type that the Sassanid Persians used in their mounted combat with the Byzantines. However, this new weapon was used in the Islamic army by infantry not cavalry. This new weapon enabled the Islamic infantry to be successful against the elephants. The elephants' long reach was too dangerous for the Muslims to attack with swords, so they simply used their spears to blind the elephants.[10] There are other non-technological reasons for Muslim success in the Battle of Badr and the Qadisiyah Campaign, however, the adoption of a new weapon, the spear, was most important. The Sassanid Persians did not use the spear in this method as their infantry was the support arm not the main arm of combat.

While the armies of Islam did attack the Sassanids directly, it was their harassment of the Sassanids from their desert sanctuary that brought down the empire. The Islamic armies used camels and their well-conditioned horses to raid Western and Persian cities for plunder. The use of cavalry raiders against the Sassanid Persians enabled the caliphs to continue their fight though the gaining of plunder and by showing the Sassanids that their government was not able to protect them. This resulted in a series of coups that would eventually bring about the end of the empire. This raiding was in keeping with the Arab method of fighting. It was not much more than an extension of their raids on caravans.

The Conquest of Egypt

The area that is modern day Syria and Iraq had been populated by Arabs prior to its occupation by the Muslim armies of the Caliph, but the Islamic invasion of Egypt broke new ground.[11] In the 600s, there were no significant Arab settlements, business, or tribes occupying the territory west of the Nile in what is modern day Egypt. The area had been fought over and plundered by Darius, and then the Sassanid Persians for hundreds of years. By the 600s, it was a Byzantine colony ruled from Alexandria by a civil governor, Cyrus, who had been proclaimed ‒Patriarch of Alexandria" by Emperor Heraclius. Cyrus ruled harshly; intolerant of any but the Empire's official Christian religion. In 639, Heraclius replaced Cyrus with a military commander who had orders to prepare Egypt for military defense.[12]

The armies of Islam continued the expansion of the Muslim empire by invading Egypt in December of 639. Muslim accounts of the conquest of Egypt begin with the Muslim commander in Gaza, Amr bin al-As, conducting a personal reconnaissance into Egypt and realizing its possibilities in terms of physical wealth for the Muslims.[13] Amr received permission from the Caliph Umar to cross into Egypt for the faith. The Muslims besieged Farama (modern Port Said) for a month and captured it.[14] The Muslims then took Bilbays and Umm Dunayn (modern day north side of Cairo vicinity Heliopolis).

According to Ibn Abd al-Hakam, the Byzantines had built a fort of earthworks and surrounded themselves with caltrops.[15] The simple fact that the Muslims were able to reduce this position shows that they had further developed some primitive siege techniques that could be used with their horse and camel-born mobile army. However, the attack does not appear to have relied on sophisticated siege equipment. The Muslims then attacked into Babylon (Old Cairo). The attack into the heart of Egypt provoked the Byzantines to action. By this time, the army of Islam had received reinforcements and totaled 12,000 against the Byzantines' 50,000 backed by a strong navy.[16] Amr, ―knowing that he lacked the equipment or technical expertise for a siege (of Babylon), attempted to lure the defenders out of their fortresses and engage them in battle in the open country."[17] Theodore, the Byzantine Emperor's appointed military commander, attacked. The armies faced each other in the same manner as in previous battles. Amr's men dismounted and fought with swords, spears, and bows against the better equipped Byzantines. Amr sent a detachment of 500 cavalrymen to the rear of the Byzantine formations and while the main party of the Byzantines fought toward their front, the ambush party attacked. The Byzantines fled to their fortress.

Amr now faced the challenge of attacking a strong position with no siege equipment save some very small towers and a few ladders.[18] Faced with a difficult military situation, Amr resorted to trickery. He enlisted the help of Copts inside the wall who had been persecuted by the Byzantines. They opened the gates and allowed the Muslim army into the city. Simultaneously, Amr's second in command, Zubayr, is reported to have scaled the walls with a small party shouting ―God is the Greatest." Upon hearing this, the defenders surrendered.[19] Technology was not key to the

30

campaign. Amr simply used guile and negotiation as well as the ⸺strength of Muslim

sword arm" in the reduction of a fortified position. While they were able to reduce a

small position, the Muslim armies, now populated by not only the Arabs, but also

increasing numbers of Persians, were not at this time capable of reducing the well made,

fortified cities of the period.[20]

The War at Sea - The Muslim Navies

The next logical step after expanding west into Egypt was to expand north. In

order to expand north, the Muslim Empire had to fight the Byzantines and that meant

creating a navy. While the early Muslim armies fought mainly on land, there was a

seafaring tradition among the Arab people.[21] The Arabs had long been sea-faring traders.

In addition, the Caliphate absorbed navies in Egypt and Syria as a defensive mechanism

against the Byzantine Empire whose reach still extended to their former lands. While

Caliph Umar (579-656) feared the sea, his successor, Caliph Uthman (581-644),

embraced it. Rather than embracing it in a Byzantine manner, he kept with Muslim

tradition--as a method for profitable raiding.

The first target of Muslim fleets was Cyprus which was raided and then

garrisoned by Muawiyah, then Governor of Syria in 649.[22] The navies of Islam had free

reign in the eastern Mediterranean until 655 when they met a large Byzantine navy off

the Lycian coast at what would later be called the Battle of the Masts. This was a

deliberate naval engagement in which Emporer Constans II chose to assemble a large

fleet to destroy the Muslim navy thus protecting his capital. Muawiyah, by now all but

the pronounced caliph and ruling from Damascus, ordered Ibn Abi Sarh, the governor of

Egypt who was also designated ⸺in charge of the sea" to intercept.[23] The navies met and agreed to a truce for the night. The Muslims had 200 ships to the Byzantine 1,000.[24] According to historian Hugh Kennedy, the two navies closed the next morning and the Muslims —grappled with the Byzantines" in a manner that looked like small land battles.[25] The navies exchanged volleys of arrows and then fought with swords and daggers and many on both sides were killed. The battle ended when the Emperor was wounded and fled the scene leaving many Byzantines to the Muslim sailors. Though historical details are not available, what is clear is that the relatively inexperienced Muslim navy defeated the best navy in the Mediterranean.

Though the Battle of the Masts was a victory, it was not decisive. The Byzantines and the Muslims continued to fight for naval supremacy and twice besieged Constantinople with naval and land forces. Both sieges failed. What is important about Muslim naval development is not that they were unsuccessful, but that the Caliphate could transform from a solely land-based military into one that could invade islands and challenge the Byzantine Empire on the Mediterranean, in a short amount of time. The Muslim Empire began as a land-based raiding force in the early 600s and seventy years later besieged its only peer competitor at Constantinople, over a thousand miles away, with a modern navy. In 670, the Ummayids conducted their first siege of Constantinople lasting until 677.[26] The only things that saved the Byzantines were the chain that safeguarded the Bosporus and their use of —Greek Fire" from the walls of Constantinople. Greek Fire at this time was not easily transportable, and the Muslims simply chose to avoid the capital until they could find a technological solution to the problem in the late 1400s. In spite of their inability to take Constantinople, the Muslims continued to raid along the coast of the Mediterranean as far as Sicily, North Africa, and even into Spain.

They had incorporated a pre-existing tradition of captured lands as Islam spread and turned it for use in their way of war--raiding for plunder and invading for the spread of the Empire.

The Continued Spread of the Empire

With the death of Uthman and then Husayn (626-680), grandson of the Prophet, Caliph Muawiya consolidated Islamic power into the new capital of Damascus. The primary threat was the Byzantines to the north and the Ummayids continued the war with the Byzantine empire. After the first unsuccessful siege of Constantinople, the Ummayids attempted again to capture Constantinople with similar results. The Caliphate continued to expand its presence in the Mediterranean as a counter to the Byzantines. The Empire also expanded into Spain and France.

The Muslim expansion into France culminated at the Battle of Poitiers. The Battle of Poitiers (732), like many others in this time period, is poorly documented. Historian Victor Davis Hanson says it happened on –probably a Saturday in October 732."[27] It is important to note that the battle happened almost exactly 100 years after the death of the Prophet. Hanson says that –the Arab conquests were a result of two phenomena; prior contact with the Byzantines, from whom they borrowed, looted, and then adapted arms, armor, and some of their military organization; and the weakness of the Persian Sassanids and the barbarian Visigoth successors in the old Roman provinces of Asia and North Africa."[28] Regardless of the technology they borrowed from the Byzantines or the fact that their enemies were weak, the Muslims conquests were also an indication of their military and political power.

At Poitiers, the Muslims assembled an army which numbered between 20,000-30,000 under Abd ar-Rahman al-Ghefiki, the military governor of Spain. They were opposed by the army of Charles ―the Hammer‖ Martel, proclaimed ―Mayor of the Palace‖ and titular head of the Franks, which also numbered about the 30,000.[29] The Muslim army contained a large number of Berbers as well as Arabs. The army of Charles Martel was a Frankish army that served Martel as the regent of the strongest Western power since the fall of Rome.

The Muslim army arrived first and immediately plundered Poitiers then burned its famous cathedral. They then turned toward Tours. The army was not as mobile as usual as it was laden with plunder and far from its base of operations. The Berbers had collected a large amount of plunder which they were unwilling to abandon to fight.[30] Upon the arrival of the Franks, the armies skirmished for seven days on the southern banks of the Loirre River with no decisive result. On the eighth day, Abd ar-Rahman took the initiative and attacked. While the armies had nearly equal numbers, they could hardly have been more different in composition, purpose, and fighting style. The Muslims utilized the same formula for battle that had worked since the days of Mohammed. They fought primarily from horseback without stirrups while the Franks formed a tight infantry formation armed with swords, shields, and spears and armored that was later called a ―wall of ice.‖[31] The Muslims simply ran into the infantry formation where the Franks solid ranks hewed them down.[32]

On the ninth day, as the armies fought each other, confusion ran rampant through the Muslim lines. The Franks had created a gap in the Muslim lines and word had spread that a large amount of plunder was about to be recaptured by the Franks. At this point, a

34

heavy cavalry force withdrew from the field without orders. The army crumbled as the Franks attacked and in the confusion, Abd ar-Rahman was killed by an arrow.

Though the actual fighting was inconclusive, there remained much confusion about what to do in the Muslim camp at the end of the day. During the night, it was decided by the Muslim leadership that, since there was no longer a central leader, the Muslims would retire from the field. Charles Martel and his army awoke to an empty Muslim camp of tents and the Muslim wounded left on the battlefield. This was the first decisive defeat of the Islamic armies since Mohammed. The Franks had checked the expansion of the Muslims into Europe.

Two concepts that were not new combined to defeat the Muslim army at Poitiers. They had seen the Sassanid Persians' heavy armor on horseback that could soften an infantry formation with arrows and then clear the battlefield of the remaining foot soldiers whether mounted or dismounted. Despite this experience, they chose not to use armor on the campaign or in their fighting method while the Franconian knights wore theirs. The Empire had also used primitive fortifications comparable to the ―wall of ice" has been compared to, had fought the disciplined infantry of the Byzantines, and could conduct missile attacks with their bows. The Muslims were unable to change their method of fighting and it cost them Europe. They had chosen to use the technology of the Persians in the form of bows and lances, but had chosen not to use armor and the Persian method of fighting that combined archer and heavy cavalryman. They were defeated by an army that the Sassanid Persians would have understood and perhaps defeated.

Manzikert – 1071 AD

The period of time between Poitiers and the rise of the Seljuq Turks when the Abbasids ruled the Muslim world from Baghdad from 750-967 is commonly called the Golden Age and it truly was. Historian Sir John Glubb calls it the ―Age of Wealth and Culture.‖ The Muslim Empire was the center of the world. The Muslim world became the center of knowledge as the Western world had entered the Dark Ages.[33] There were threats to the north in the form of the Byzantines and internal threats, but largely, the Abbasids ruled without much turmoil. The end of the Abbasid Empire would not be turmoil free. In its last years, the Empire suffered coups, assassinations, and near civil war. By 975, the Byzantines had reconquered their previously occupied portions of the Middle East including Syria.

The Abbasids ruled the Middle East and loosely North Africa and Spain. Their army of varied races was united by one common trait: Islam. The large army's components took on regional characteristics. For example, the army of the east was predominately from steppe people with fewer Arabs than most other ethnic groups. In the west, the army was comprised of Arabs, Egyptians, Algerians, and Moors. That diversity in ethnicity was evident in the army that campaigned in Spain and France. The historian Ahmed ibn Mohammed al-Maqqari described the Islamic solider who fought in Spain at the turn of the millennium by saying that they wore ―a dress very similar to that of the Christians, their neighbors. They used similiar weapons, and, like them, were clad in mail, over which they threw a short scarlet tunic, in the Christian fashion.‖[34]

The Abbasid Empire would end in an assumption of power by the rise of a Turkish family, the Ghuzz. The Ghuzz formed the nucleus of what is now called the

—Seljuq Turks." The Seljuqs first order of business was to remove the Byzantines from the Middle East. They did so by attacking and plundering the plateaus of Cicilia, Phrygia, and Galatia while simultaneously invading Asia Minor.[35] Emperor Romanus sent forces against both columns. The eastern armies battled indecisively for two years until the Byzantines won at Trebizond in 1068. The western armies met in 1071 at Manzikert.[36] Romanus brought with him a mixed race army or Bulgars, Greeks, Armenians, Slavs, Goths, and Georgians as well as a number of non-Muslim Turks. His army numbered nearly 200,000 with 4,000 carts for armaments and numerous catapults.[37] It is unclear as to the size of the Muslim army. The Muslims met the Byzantines on the field on a Friday afternoon after prayer. On August 25, the emperor's troops made contact with the Seljuqs. On August 26, the emperor gathered his army into formation and marched and rode on the Seljuq positions. The Byzantine army was divided into three wings with the left and right under trusted subordinates and the center commanded by the emperor himself. The Seljuqs formed into a crescent about four kilometers away from the Byzantines with their commander observing away from the main battle area. Seljuq horse archers fired at the Byzantines' wings as they moved forward. While the Byzantines moved forward, the Seljuq center moved backward while the wings held. By the afternoon, the Byzantines had captured Alp Arslan's camp; however, this was irrelevant. The Seljuqs' arrow attacks against the Byzantines had achieved their purpose, and the wings broke under relatively light pressure from the Seljuqs. Romanus was forced to order a withdrawal prior to nightfall. Unfortunately, the right wing did not get the order and the left wing turned back to camp. The Seljuqs seized the initiative and in

37

very little time, the center was surrounded. The emperor was captured and the battle was ended.[38]

The Seljuq warrior was mounted, wore very little if any body armor, and carried a slightly curved saber. He might carry a javelin as a secondary weapon, but his primary weapon a short composite bow and thirty to fifty arrows. The bow was a laminated recurve with sinew on the back and horn on the belly which gave it tremendous power despite its small size. His bow gave him the ability to take quick shots or long distance shots at his enemy. His mobility came from his horse. He would fire his bow and then retreat to turn and fire again and again. This method of fighting looks again much like the Parthians without the heavy cavalry to press the attack home. There was a Parthian shot with no following attack.

The Mamluks – the Epitome of Islam at War

The Mamluks, the word for slave in Arabic, came into the Islamic world to fill the need for an army loyal only to the caliph. Up to this point, the army of Islam had gone from almost exclusively Arab to a mix of Arab, Berber, Kurd, Persian, and others. The army had no racial core. Caliph al-Mamun, an Abbasid Caliph, (r. 813-33) had to pay off the Khurasanis to remain part of his army during a civil war within Islam.[39] Al-Mamun had to create an army loyal only to him. He chose to build an army of slaves. These slaves were abducted, sold, and bought as children. Training began at adolescence and ensured loyalty to the caliph and not to any tribe. The Abbasids began buying boys from the steppes of Central Asia and southern Russia on a large scale. There are many reasons why: the lands from which they came were harsh and thus they were hardier than the Arabs or Khurasanis; steppe children grew up on horseback and could function extremely well in the cavalry-based Muslim armies; and most importantly, they were plentiful and, in many cases, not wanted and therefore cheap.[40] With the creation of the Mamluks, the caliphs had what they thought was the ultimate army.

The Mamluks grew to form the elite of the Muslim armies. They fought at Manzikert, Hattim, and nearly every battle in Muslim history from the time of Mamluk inception. They were loyal to the caliph and were passed as an intact army from the Abbasids to the Seljuqs and to the Muwahhids. By the 1220s, the Islamic was split into four main factions: the Abbasids, who had risen again, in Baghdad; the Ayoubids ruling from Cairo; the Khuwarizm Shahs in Persia; and the Seljuq Turks, who still held Asia Minor. Not only did they have to contend with each other and the Crusaders, but there was a great new threat on the rise--the Mongols. In 1220, Jenghis Khan's armies took Bukhara and Samarqand in modern day Iran. While his death in 1227 took some of the pressure off the Muslim world, it was not completely gone.

When the Mongols resumed operations, the Seljuqs fell first and became a tributary in 1243. The western Persians fell next followed by the Abbasids. The Mongols sacked Baghdad in 1258. By 1260, the Ayoubids were the only Muslim nation still able to fight the Mongols.

After a struggle for power lasting several years, Qutuz, a Mamluk general, became sultan of the new Mamluk state. He took control just in time to meet the renewed Mongol Offensive. Fortunately for the Mamluks, in 1260, the Great Khan Mangu died and his brother, Hulagu, the conqueror of Baghdad who was leading the offensive toward Cairo, immediately departed for China to attempt to become Khan and left his army in the care of Kit Buqa a less competent commander.

39

On September 3, 1260, the Mamluks under Qutuz met the Mongols at a field eleven miles southwest of Nazareth called Ain Jaloot--Goliath's Spring.[41] In a surprising turn of events, the Crusaders actually aided the Mamluks with food and other facilities.[42] The Mongols had lost their leader to an internal struggle while the Mamluks had their first Sultan at the head of their army. The Mongols were fighting away from their bases while the Mamluks were fighting in their nation and had allied support. The Mamluks under Baybars the Bunduqdari, the Mamluk second in command, met and defeated the forward detachment of the Mongols and the Mongol second in command, Baydar, at Gaza.[43] The Mamluks continued and defeated the Mongol local reconnaissance force at Ain Jaloot on September 3, 1260. This left Kit Buqa blind to the numbers of the Mamluk army. While the Mamluk army was slightly smaller than the Mongols, it was homogenous while the Mongol army contained a large number of Georgians and Armenians that was not as bonded as the Mamluk army.[44] On September 3, the Mongols took position first and the Mamluks attacked. The Mongols defeated the Mamluk left flank easily until the personal appearance of Qutuz rallied the Mamluks. This combined with the desertion of the Mongols allies, the Ayyubids, turned the tide of the battle in favor of the Mamluks. The Mongols were defeated and Kit Buqa was either killed outright or captured and then beheaded. The defeat of the Mamluks at Ain Jaloot ended Mongol military operations in the region.

This victory is another indication of the prowess of Islamic armies in the Middle Ages. The Mamluks did use their superb archery skills combined with one of the best bows in existence at the time to defeat the Mongols, but the Mongols had a similar bow.

It was not the use of the bow that won the day, but the use of general purpose cavalry that won the battle and the war against the Mongols.

The Mamluks not only demonstrated superb capability as mobile cavalry, they also brought into the Muslim army siege machines. While siege machines had been in existence for a great amount of time, they had been sparse in Muslim armies. This was due to the need for swift attacks and an ability to retreat into the desert if need be. The Mamluks brought the trebuchet to the Middle East.[45] In 1285, the Mamluk Sultan Qalawun besieged the Hospitaller fortress of al-Marqab (Margat) with three *qarabughra*, three *bricola*s, identified as "Frankish" or "European" trebuchets, and four traction trebuchets.[46] The Mamluks besieged the town of Acre in 1291 with a bombardment that lasted six weeks and involved 90 mangonels--the largest number ever assembled against the walls of any Middle Eastern city.[47] As the Muslims reduced a wall, they then filled in the defensive trenches between the walls of the city to continue the movement of their siege engines forward. The final step was an assault against the city that resulted in the Mamluks gaining entry to the inner walls. After a truce was refused by the Templars, the Mamluks continued the barrage and captured the city.

If the Mamluks were so advanced and could refine the technology, concepts, and tactics as seen in their use of not only mobile, armored, multi-purpose cavalry and trebuchets why were they defeated by the Ottomans so easily in 1517. The answer is much simpler than culture. It was an arms race that the Mamluks simply could not win. The greatest quality of the Mamluk, extensive and expensive training, was negated by a trained soldier with a gun. This is the same fault of the armored knight of Europe. This is not to say that the Mamuks ignored firearms. There were cannon on the walls of the

41

Mamluk fortresses at Kerak and Damascus in 1342 and 1352 respectively.[48] These dates

correspond relatively to 40 years after cannon made their debut in Europe and 60 years

prior to the first reports of cannon in the Ottoman Empire.[49] The Mamluks understood

what the firearms of the day could do; what they misunderstood was that it signaled the

end of the armored knight. Historian David Ayalon posits that the Mamluks did without

firearms until it was too late because they could —arry on quite comfortably without

them."[50] The Mamluks had perfected the non-gunpowder propelled siege machine to the

point that they could mass it better than the Europeans. However, when faced with a

death struggle with the Ottomans to the north and the Portuguese to the southeast, the

Mamluks decided, although belatedly, to accept firearms. The Mamluks accepted them

within the construct of traditional Mamluk methods of warfare.[51] While the Mamluks

began producing cannon at an unheard of rate, there was no plan from the Sultan on how

to use them other than for defense of the Mediterranean coast. Unfortunately, the threat

was to the east and southeast.

Prior to their ascension into the sultanate, the Mamluks were the best soldiers in

the Muslim empire and perhaps the world. They had been chosen from the slave yards

and studied warfare for their entire lives. After their initial successes, the training of the

Mamluk soldier lessened in quality and quantity due to nothing other than neglect by the

Mamluks in power. Sultan al-Gahwri brought that training back to the forefront but

again, it was too little too late and too focused on lance, sword, and bow.[52] The Mamluk

army in 1500, particularly Mamluk units, looked in equipment and fighting method

exactly as they had 100 and 200 years prior. The problem lay not in the equipment. It

lay in the mentality of the Mamluk. The Mamluk, who came from steppe people, chose not to use the cannon because it required a specialist from outside of the Mamluk ranks and did not affect their construct of war. However, the Mamluks in general refused to carry the harquebus because it not only replaced their bow, but also threatened the horse and thus horse cavalry.[53] This was a deliberate cultural, not religious, decision on the part of the Mamluks. Horse archers were so deeply rooted in their culture that they could evolve into an infantry army. The result was a defeat first at Marj Dabij, north of Aleppo, in 1516 in which the Mamluks charged cannon and were repulsed and then defeated. Their sultan was killed on the battlefield. Then followed a defeat at al-Radaniyya that continued the pyramids of Giza on January 23, 1517 in which the Mamluks lost their empire to the Ottomans.[54]

Islamic Armies Fighting Method Remained the Same

From the early days of Islam, technology increased the effectiveness of Islamic armies: better weapons, ships as a means of plundering, siege techniques, European style armor, and finally firearms. The Islamic army of Badr looked nothing like the army of the Mamluks at Cairo and not only for technological reasons. The armies of Islam began as caravan raiding mobs and turned into the most professionally trained army of the day. In fact, the Mamluks were so proficient that they could not adopt firearms as their primary weapon system as a replacement for the bow. The armies of the caliphs were able to take the spear from the Sassanids and apply it to kill their elephants. The armies of the Abbasids took the naval capabilities of the peoples of the Mediterranean coast and nearly brought Constantinople to its end. The Abbasids and their Mamluk cavalry then began to look like the Crusaders in armor and equipment, but did not use that equipment in the same manner. The sword remained the secondary weapon in favor of the bow.

Despite advances in technology, the basic approach to fighting remained the same. The Mamluks last charge at Giza –set a volley of arrows flying before charging with their lances crouched" into the Ottoman cannons.[55] The fact that even though the infantry based army of the Franks defeated the Islamic army at Poitiers with no change in fighting doctrine shows how wed the Muslims were to their cavalry. To do otherwise would be breaking from the tradition of the Prophet.

---

[1]A Kharijite is a described by historian Bernard Lewis as a Muslim group that split from the party of Ali ibn Alit Talib. The word is a derivative of the Arabic for –to go out." According to Lewis, the Kharijites represented the most extreme form of tribal independence; they refused to accept any authority not deriving from their own freely given and always revocable consent, an insisted that any believer, of whatever birth and origin, could be caliph if chosen by the believers." Bernard Lewis, *The Middle East* (New York: Scribener Press, 1995), 66.

[2]While upon the death of Ali in 661, it was not until he defeat in battle and death of Husayn at the Battle of Karbala (October 9 or 10, 680) that the establishment of the Ummayid caliphate was complete. The transfer of leadership from the Prophet to Muawiyah is described in many books, however, the best is Sir Phillip Glubb, *A Short History of the Arab Peoples* (New York: Stein and Day, 1969).

[3]Oliver Lyman Spaulding and Hoffman Nickerson, *Ancient and Medieval Warfare* (New York: Barnes and Noble Books, 1993), 274.

[4]Ibid.

[5]George F. Nafzinger and Mark W. Walton, *Islam at War: A History* (Weston, CT: Praegar Press, 2003), 23.

[6]Siddiqi describes the start of almost every battle in the Great Conquests period as beginning with individual, champion style-combat. Amir H.Siddiqi, *Decisive Battles of Islam* (Lahore, Pakistan: Islamic Book Publishers, 1986), 9-10.

[7]Ibid., 37,

[8]Medina in much of the literature is known as Yathrib to the point when the Prophet fled there. Thereafter it as known as Medinat al-Nebi or the City of the Prophet. Ibid., 34.

[9]Ibid., 35.

[10]Ibid., 48.

[11]Hugh Kennedy, *Great Arab Conquests: How the Spread of Islam Changed the World We Live in* (Philadelphia: Da Capo Press, 2007), 139.

[12]Ibid., 146.

[13]Ibid. The text tells a story in which Amr saves the life of a passing Christian on his way to the Church of the Holy Sepulcher. After Amr saves his life, the deacon takes Amr to Egypt as his guest where Amr witnesses firsthand the riches of Egypt. He then decides to invade.

[14]Ibid., 148. The text lists that there are no further details in history other than the Muslims besieged it and captured it within a month.

[15]Futūh, 56. Ibid.

[16]Glubb, *A Short History of the Arab Peoples* (New York: Stein and Day Publishers, 1969), 51. Hitti also points out that the Muslims did not have a single ship nor any siege machines.

[17]Kennedy, *Great Arab Conquests*, 151.

[18]Ibid., 152.

[19]The taking of the city is similar to the taking of Damascus by Khalid bin al-Walid and shows, if true, the use of siege technology in keeping with Muslim tradition. Glubb, *A Short History of the Arab Peoples*, 48.

[20]While the Muslims may have been able to siege a city and reduce it through guile, it is highly unlikely that they could reduce a European castle of this period given their lack of siege engines and thus siege doctrine and tactics.

[21]Kennedy, *Great Arab Conquests*, 326.

[22]Ibid. The Koran (Surah 30:46) tells the faithful that God sent the winds –so that the ship may sail at His command and so that you may seek of His bounty."

[23]Ibid., 327. This battle is described by both the Greek Chronicle of Theophanes and the Arabic chronicle of Ibn al-Athir and due to these works is the most well documented naval battle of the period according to Kennedy. However since it is only two sources, it again shows the relatively small amount of information on these battles.

[24]Ibid., 328. Ibn Abd al-Hakam's figure.

[25]Ibid., 327.

[26]This is depicted in Glubb, *A Short History of the Arab Peoples*. The second siege was also unsuccessful for similar reasons and occurred from 716-717.

[27]Hanson, *Carnage and Culture*, 141.

[28]Ibid., 146.

[29]These numbers come from Hanson's Carnage and Culture. There are conflicting numbers in several accounts from tens of thousands to hundreds of thousands in difference. Historian Paul K. Davis writes that the numbers were closer to 30,000 Franks and 80,000 Berbers and Arabs.

[30]Both facts come from Siddiqi, *Decisive Battles of Islam*, 95.

[31]The Mozarabic Chronicle of 754 says: —Ad in the shock of the battle the men of the North seemed like a sea that cannot be moved. Firmly they stood, one close to another, forming as it were a bulwark of ice; and with great blows of their swords they hewed down the Arabs. Drawn up in a band around their chief, the people of the Austrasians carried all before them. Their tireless hands drove their swords down to the breasts of the foe." William Stearns Davis, ed., Readings in Ancient History: Illustrative Extracts from the Sources, 2 Vols. (Boston: Allyn and Bacon, 1912-13), Vol. II: Rome and the West, 362-364, http://www.fordham.edu/halsall/source/732tours.html (accessed April 16, 2009).

[32]Hitti, *The Arabs: A Short History*, 70.

[33]In Baghdad, everything was covered in gold from buildings to belt buckles. Conversation and culture were considered became art while intellectual discussions permeated the educated class. Poetry remained —the typical Arab art form and was sedulously practiced." Glubb, *A Short History of the Arab Peoples*, 105.

[34]He goes on to say that the —Andalusian troops were again clad and armed in the real Arabic fashion; instead of the heavy steel helmet and thick breast-plate of their ancestors; they wore a slender head-piece, and a thin but well-tempered cuirass; instead of the huge spear with a broad end in the Christian fashion, they took the long and slender reed of the Arabs, and they substituted for the clumsy and ill-shaped Christian saddles the more military-looking and more convenient horse furniture of the inhabitants of Arabia." Ahmed Ibn Mohammed Al-Maqqari, *The History of the Mohammedan Dynasties in Spain*, translated by Pascual de Gayangos, 2 volumes (London: Oriental Translation Fund), 1840.

[35]Glubb, *A Short History of the Arab Peoples*, 99.

[36]Also called Malazikert or Malazgirt.

[37]Siddiqi, *Decisive Battles of Islam*, 100.

[38]Brian T. Carey, ―Debacle at Manzikert, 1071: A Prelude to the Crusades,‖ Medieval History, from http://www.deremilitarrii.org (accessed February 1, 2009).

[39]James Waterson, *The Knights of Islam: The Wars of the Mamluks* (London: Greenhill Books, 2007), 37.

[40]Ibid., 38.

[41]Some sources quote September 3 while others 13.

[42]Glubb, *A Short History of the Arab Peoples*, 208.

[43]Baybers is acknowledged as the founder of the Mamluk Sultanate. He would later murder Sultan Qutuz on the march back to Cairo and proclaim himself Sultan. Waterson, *The Knights of Islam*, 76.

[44]Ibid., 78.

[45]Paul E. Chevedden, ―Black Camels and Blazing Bolts: The Bolt-Projecting Trebuchet in the Mamluk Army,‖ *Mamluk Studies Review* 8, no. 1 (2004): 244-245.

[46]Ibid., 247.

[47]Waterson, *The Knights of Islam*, 194.

[48]David Ayalon, *Gunpowder and Firearms in the Mamluk Kingdom: A Challenge to a Mediaeval Society* (London: Frank Cass Publishing, 1956), 2.

[49]Ibid., 4.

[50]Ibid.

[51]This is a decision made by Sultan al-Ghawri (r. 1500-1516). His plan was threefold: (1) Cast a considerable amount of new cannon, (2) Renew furusiya (the Mamluk method of training exercises) and the traditional art of war, and (3) Raise a unit of harquibusiers. These harquibusiers were auxiliary foot soldiers and still considered beneath the Mamluk cavalry. Ibid., 48.

[52]Ibid., 52.

[53]Ibid., 60. Ayalon describes this extremely well when he discusses the ability to leverage specialists but not to change the general purpose heavy cavalry that the Mamluks were so famous for employing.

[54]Waterson, *The Knights of Islam*, 283-4.

[55]Ibid., 284.

CHAPTER 4

THE RISE AND FALL OF THE OTTOMANS

The Islamic domination of the Middle East, North Africa, and Central Asia continued from the Middle Ages through the early 20th Century. The primary land holder was the Ottoman Empire from its capital in Istanbul. The period of 1500-1918 saw the rise of the nation-state, professional armies, and the introduction and refinement of gunpowder weapons large and small. It is in this period that the empires, and later nations, of Islam failed to capitalize on previous successes and thus doomed themselves to second-rate power status behind their Western competitors. This chapter will discuss the general history of the Ottomans, the Battle of Kosovo, the rise of the professional army, the continued development of a Muslim navy, and the development and use of firearms.

General History

After the fall of the Seljuks and with their reduction of the Mamluk Empire in 1517, the Ottomans unified the East. The Seljuks had conquered most of Iraq as well as a portion of Anatolia before their fall to the Mongols in 1300. In their place rose Yavlak Arslan and later his son, Ali (combined rule 1284-1299), the rulers of a small principality in Anatolia. Arslan was able to maintain his rule through cooperation with both the Mongols and the Byzantines. At his death, his son Ali conquered Byzantine territory to the Sakayra River. When Ali decided to ally himself with the Byzantines, Osman Bey (or Osman I, r 1317-1326), a member of another tribe and the founder of the Ottoman Dynasty, occupied several key forts from the Seljuks that controlled terrain from Anatoia to the plains of Bithynia. This created the Ottoman Empire. Osman then put the Byzantine city of Bursa under siege in 1317 and it fell in 1326. The Byzantines launched a major expedition against Osman in 1328 with Emperor Andronicus III (r 1328-41) personally in command. The Ottomans routed the Byzantines at the Battle of Pelecanon and forced the Emperor back into Constantinople enabling the Ottomans to isolate Constantinople and attack into Europe.

The Ottomans attacked into Europe and conquered the coastal region north of Constantinople. The Ottomans, having been asked for assistance by the current Byzantine Emperor, John V Palaeolgus (r), assisted the Byzantines in their pacification of the Balkans by occupying them and eventually establishing a permanent garrison at Gallipoli in 1354.[1] Since the Byzantines were unable to control their lands to the north due to lack of military power and recent coups, Emperor John V Palaeolgus allied himself with the Ottomans. This enabled the Ottomans to gain peaceful access to the land north of the Bosporus.

The Battle for Kosovo

The Battle of Kosovo (or Kosovo Polje--the Plain of Blackbirds) was the largest battle in the campaign to establish Ottoman control of the Balkans and serves as a model for how the Ottoman Empire fought.[2] The Battle for Kosovo was fought on either June 15th or June 28th, 1389 in a field about five kilometers north of Pristina. Sultan Murad I (r. 1359-1389) commanded the army of 27-40,000 Ottomans in their campaign to occupy Kosovo. This campaign continued the encroachment on the territory of the Byzantine Empire. The army of 12-30,000 Serbs was commanded by Prince Lazar Hrebeljanovic who had defeated Murad before at the Battle of Plocnik.[3]

Both armies lined up for battle with the Ottomans to the north and the Serbs to the south. Murad occupied the center of the Ottoman formation where he could observe the entire battle with his son Bayezid (r 1389-1402) on his right and his other son, Yakub, on his left. The Ottoman army formed into lines with archers on the wings, European vassals on the right, Janissaries in the center, and Anatolia Ottomans on the left.[4]

While there are conflicting reports to the details of the battle, the general scheme holds that the two armies charged each other with the Serbs nearly defeating the Ottomans. Bayezid's personal charge into the Serbian knights inspired the Ottomans to victory. In the confusion of the battle, a knight was able to assassinate Sultan Murad through either hiding in corpses or feigning surrender. While dying, Sultan Murad ordered his reserve to pursue the Serbs. The reserve captured King Lazar and brought him before the dying Sultan Murad where he was executed.[5] Once this was done, the Serbs collapsed and the battle turned into a rout. The Ottomans killed the remainder of the Serbs turning the battlefield into ―the Field of Blackbirds" named for the ravens that feasted on its dead.[6]

This battle is significant because the Ottomans demonstrated continuity. Continuity is represented by a strong land based army; an army whose core was a slave-based corps, the Janissaries (much like the Mamluks). The horse cavalryman remained the primary soldier of the army. The archer continued to prepare the enemy for a charge and the cavalry remained the decisive act of battle. The Battle of Kosovo demonstrated the same arms and tactics used by the pre-modern Muslim armies.

The Establishment of a Professional Soldier and Army

The rise of the professional soldier in the Ottoman Empire came after the defeat of Beyezid I, son of Murad I, at the hands of Timur the Lame (Tamerlane) in 1402 at the Battle of Ankara.[7] In order to consolidate power, Beyezid took it from the tribal chiefs.[8] These tribal chiefs then revolted and Beyezid defeated them by means of recruiting Christian troops in one instance. After Kosovo, Beyezid was defeated in a battle against Tamerlane in which the tribal chiefs assisted Tamerlane. While in exile, Beyezid realized that the Ottomans needed an army that was loyal to him; he chose to create one based around the Janissaries.

His father, Murad I, created the Janissaries. The Ottoman army was formed from Turkomen light horsemen, *ghazis*, organized by tribes and clans under the command of the tribal chiefs and religious leaders. They were comprised almost exclusively of horse archers.[9] The use of these indisciplined irregulars prevented their employment in siege operations against walled cities and fortresses. Their dependence on plunder as a means of pay also prevented them from being used in areas that the empire was trying to cultivate. Although they could be used in overwhelming enemy field armies and in pursuit of a beaten enemy, their nature ran contrary to the Ottoman desire to establish settlements in conquered areas and thus they were relegated to border duty and raiding Christian areas.[10]

Before the Ottomans could push the Turkomen to the periphery of the army and the empire, they needed to create a replacement to continue serving as the agent of conquest and defense of the empire. Sultan Orghan Gazi (r 1324-1359) began the Ottoman process of creating a standing army manned by regular, salaried bodies of soldiers.[11] He created an army of infantry called *yaya*, and cavalry called *müsellems*, of

both Muslim and Christian Turk origin. Murad I ascended at the death of Orghan as

Orghan's son Suleiman had preceded his father in death. In his invasion of Kosovo,

Murad shifted away from the empire's use of Turkomen, relegating them to the frontiers

as shock troops (*akinci*--raiders and *deli*--fanatics) and using the standing army as his

base.[12]

In order to gain an even stronger hold over the mercenary army of the Empire,

Murad created a new organization called the "slaves of the Porte" (*kapiskullari*) who

came into the empire's service (as slaves) as young men.[13] They were educated in the

Turkish language and Ottoman culture. Many became clerks in the imperial court, but

the strongest and bravest became known as the Janissaries.[14] The Janissaries received

military training in addition to their enculturation, were organized into infantry or cavalry

known as "spahis," and were paid by and under the direct control of the Sultan.[15] With

the introduction of the Janissaries, the *yayas* and *müsellems* assumed rear-area duties

while the Janissaries became the primary instrument of conquest. The Ottoman Empire

had a professional albeit relatively small army but was able to dominate most of Eastern

Europe and the Middle East for over a century.

The Janissaries served the Ottomans much in the same manner as the Mamluks

had served the Abbasids for over 200 years. The ranks of the Janissaries and the

conscripted army swelled in the following centuries into a large and magnificent army. It

has been called "certainly the largest, and at its core also the finest in the Eurasian

world."[16] After the Europeans defeated Suleiman the Magnificent and his army in 1529

at Vienna, the Ottoman army failed to change. Most of the army remained little more than a conscripted levy without the drill or discipline that was key to the conflicts of the period. Their tactics and methods remained grounded in the pre-Vienna era. The Janissaries remained at the core of the army, but their increasing influence on the political side of the empire forced the Sultan to take actions against them.[17] In 1825-6, the Janissaries attacked and pillaged most of Constantinople in response to Sultan Mahmud II's *fatwa* that it was the duty of all Muslims to serve in the Ottoman military. The Janissaries were then surrounded by other Ottoman forces and slaughtered. This decreased the military value of the army even further. Prior to the removal of the Janissaries, British General John Moore in 1801 had described the existing Ottoman army that had defeated Napoleon at Acre in 1799 a ―wild, ungoverned mob.‖[18]

The army only worsened after the removal of the Janissaries in 1826. During World War I army leadership was so poor that the Ottomans appointed German General Liman von Sanders as the commander-in-chief of Turkish armed forces. Another German field marshal was given command of all Turkish forces in Mesopotamia.[19] German generals and officers filled many other key command and staff positions throughout the war.

Leadership was crucial to the decline of the Ottoman army, but the reluctance of the Ottomans to utilize gunpowder weapons in a manner similar to the Europeans was another contributing factor. It was gunpowder that created the largest rift in the parity between Europe and the Ottomans. This was seen in naval combat at Lepanto and was present in every land based battle that the Ottomans fought.

The Ottomans gave credence to the individual warrior and his bravery in battle because his entrance into heaven depended on it. Historian Andrew Wheatcroft states that instead of using musketry *en masse*, as was developing in the West, or massed pikemen acting in unison, the Ottomans looked upon each musketeer or sharpshooter as a warrior risking his life for a place in paradise."[20] The Ottomans chose to use firearms but could not manufacture them. Their usage began at the Siege of Constantinople.

The Ottomans consolidated power in Asia Minor and spent decades plundering the Balkans. The Byzantines controlled little outside their own walls. They formed alliances with the Ottomans to retain what they did control. The Ottomans had a permanent settlement in Gallipoli. The Sultan needed to destroy the Byzantines once and for all and that meant capturing Constantinople. The Seljuks and Ottomans had sieged Constantinople several times before 1453. Each time, they had to abandon the siege due to the end of the campaign season. They had been unable to break the walls due to limited siege equipment. The introduction of the bombard changed this.

The bombard came to the Ottomans from a Hungarian gun founder named Urban who abandoned his employment with the Byzantines over a pay dispute.[21] By this point in time, it is likely that the Ottomans had some bombards in their inventory. What Urban created for the Sultan was a bombard so large that it fired stone balls that weighed twelve hundred pounds. The bombard was said to be almost nine meters long, had eight inch thick walls, and a thirty inch bore.[22] It was able to propel a twelve hundred pound stone over a mile and create a crater six feet deep.[23] Once the bombard was in place, the siege began and over a period of fifty-five days the bombards fired 100 to 120 times per day literally tearing the walls of Constantinople apart and enabling the Ottomans to breach, capture, and pillage the city thus finally ending the empire.[24] While it is important to note the superior Ottoman technology, it is more important to note that it came from a

European because it shows a lack of technological ability and possibly imagination to build a bombard necessary to ensure the final destruction of the primary enemy of the Ottoman Empire.

Many point to the Ottoman use of firearms against the Mamluks in 1516 at the Battle of Aleppo as evidence of Ottoman reception and Mamluk rejection of hand-held firearms.[25] However, the common firearm at this time had less range and poorer accuracy than the Mamluk compound bow and had a rate of fire four times faster.[26] It was not Ottoman use of hand-held firearms that enabled them to defeat the Mamluks, rather the Ottomans defeated the Mamluks with artillery that had been adapted from the 1453 Siege of Constantinople. What is important to note is that the Ottomans used a new technology while the Mamluks deliberately chose to remain a bow-based army.

The Ottomans lacked the capability to manufacture bombard, artillery, and hand firearms. In 1453, the Ottomans were relying on Europeans to manufacture their firearms or were using inferior firearms and strength of arm because they were unable or unwilling to make them. One explanation for this lack of ability to use but not create new gunpowder technology is Europe's political and geographical fragmentation spurred a European arms race. Another explanation is the freer and less regulated European markets provided greater incentives for innovation.[27]

Firearms training required two components. First, the firearm-based army needed a warrior ethos to stand and fire while being fired upon. The Ottoman Army could produce that easily. Second, that army needed to conduct unit training to mass fires. Since, as Wheatcroft establishes, the Ottoman warrior risked his life for a place in heaven, he was more likely to perform as an individual than as a member of a formation. This unit training was counter to Islamic and thus Ottoman culture.

The lack of a professional army and the failure to capitalize on the use of gunpowder weapons were two military reasons for the decline of the Ottoman Empire. The Janissaries predated the modern professional army by nearly two centuries. Rather than capitalizing on the professionalism of that core, the Ottomans continued to use poorly-trained and disciplined soldiers to fill out the remainder of the army. The Chinese created gunpowder weapons and they flowed through the Ottoman Empire to Europe where they were refined and used to their fullest potential while the Ottomans remained on the periphery of gunpowder technology. Those choices cost them their gains in Europe, victory in World War I, and eventually the entire Empire.

The Continued Development of a Navy

On October 7th, 1571, the combined fleet of the Ottoman Empire clashed with the joined forces of Spain, Venice, and the Holy See under the shared tactical command of Spanish prince Don Juan, Venetian Sebastian Veniero, and papal captain Marcantonio Colonna.[28] Ottoman admiral Müezzinzade Ali Pasha's fleet of war galleys faced the western fleet of galleys and a new ship, the galleass, with its 50 gun array.[29] The galleasses attacked in the front of the Christian formations of Don Juan devastating the Ottoman lines of galleys. Don Juan commanded six galleasses, but the right flank two were not able to come into battle in time. The four galleasses that participated in the naval battle destroyed ship after ship with their guns. Armed with cannons on every surface that could sustain the weight, one galleass contained the firepower of twelve galleys.[30] The Christian fleet closed with the Ottomans and began to attack the Ottomans with harquebus fire at ranges of four and five hundred yards before the Ottoman Navy could return fire with their bows. When the Ottomans finally reached a distance in which they could engage with their bows, they fired until their quivers were empty and then closed to board the Christian ships. The Christians overwhelmed the Ottomans on the decks with more harquebus fire. The Ottomans were simply outclassed. In a mere four hours, the Ottoman Navy was smashed and its admiral dead. The Ottoman reliance on outdated galleys, bows, and untrained sailors resulted in their loss at Lepanto.

The Ottomans inherited the eastern Mediterranean Sea as their own at the sudden collapse of the Byzantine Empire. The Muslim navies of the Abbasids and the Mamluks were only used to ferry troops to conquer islands or to move across bodies of water inside the Mediterranean. With Orhan's capture of Gallipoli, the Ottomans faced a new foe in the Italians. Orhan's methods of seafaring were little different from their predecessors and the *ghazis* of the land army quickly became *azebs* on board ships.[31] They had no formal training in seamanship and were drawn from the same volunteers as in the horse cavalry. The Ottomans relied on native Greeks, Christians, and the converted population of the eastern Mediterranean for specific maritime knowledge. Native Greeks constituted the professional crews of the first Ottoman ships while others were manned completely by Greeks who operated as corsairs in the service of the Sultan.[32] These Greek corsairs simply switched their allegiance from the Byzantines to the Ottomans. The majority of the great admirals of the Ottoman Empire also came from Greek stock including Hayreddin Barbarossa who became the ruler of Algiers.

The Ottoman Navy started strong by defeating the Byzantines in conjunction with the land based army. The Ottomans turned west toward the Spanish Hapsburgs and

58

established colonies by conquest in much of North Africa. In 1534, the Ottomans captured Tunis and in 1551, Tripoli. The primary ship of the Ottomans was the war galley, a relatively fast and maneuverable ship that was relatively fragile and could not withstand rough winter seas.[33] It had a small hold that could only keep enough provisions for a ten day sea voyage. The war galley's range drove the conquest of ports as ports provided sustainment for the expansion of the Ottoman Empire or the Spanish Hapsburgs.

Galley warfare was increasingly expensive. The galley itself needed men to crew it and men to crew its expanding gun array. The move to larger and larger ships created a need for more men to crew the ship and guns until the ships eventually became so expensive that both the Spanish Hapsburgs and the Ottomans could no longer afford to conduct the back and forth conquest of the Mediterranean and its islands. The Ottomans continued to turn to the Greeks for experienced sailors and they came at a high price. While some historians argue that the victory at Lepanto was decisive to the halting of Ottoman expansion, many others cite the cost of galley warfare and the limited gain of warfare on the sea as a reason for the halting of expansion on both sides. Regardless of the reasons for the halting of expansion, the price of naval warfare was another reason why Ottoman naval development remained behind Europe.

Conclusion

During the Ottoman reign there was insufficient transformation in technology, tactics, and concepts relative to their European and Persain rivals. The Ottomans failed to create a professional army that could use firearms effectively or was well led. In addition, they failed to create a professional navy to counter the expansion of Europe to the East. Therefore, by 1566, the Ottoman Empire was no match for a modern competitor.

From the period of the —Golden Age" of Islam to the dawn of the modern Arab state, the Ottoman Empire reigned as the protector of Islam. Among the many distinguished leaders, the Ottomans were led by Mehmed II, the Conqueror of Constantinople, and Suleiman the Magnificent. Wielding technology never before seen in the East and fielding huge land and sea forces, they were the dominant Middle Eastern power for over four-hundred years. They brought the professional soldier and military reform to the region to keep pace with the Europeans. The Ottomans remained a nation of sea-faring raiders vice sea conquerors. They would conquer the cavalry-based Mamluks, but would fail to capitalize on the firearm as a weapon like the Europeans. All of this combined with the incessant corruption of the Empire would weaken the Empire until it became the —Sick Old Man of Europe" that could do little during World War I.

---

[1]There are several good sources for information on the early Ottomans, but this paragraph's details come from Peter Sugar, *Southeastern Europe Under Ottoman Rule, 1354-1804* (University of Washington Press, Seattle, 1977) http://coursea. matrix.msu.edu/~fisher/hst373/readings/sugar.html (accessed April 20, 2009).

[2]Ibid.

[3]Ibid.

[4]Nafzinger and Walton, *Islam at War*, 96.

[5]Ibid.

[6]Ibid.

[7]Lewis, *The Middle East*, 102.

[8]Ibid., 47.

[9]Ibid., 94.

[10]Ibid.

[11]Ibid., 95.

[12]Ibid.

[13]Ibid. Nafzinger further describes them on 110 in which he says that —They were first organized in 1330 and annually received 1,000 twelve-year old Christian boys from the Balkans as a slave tribute to fill their ranks.

[14]Ibid.

[15]Ibid.

[16]Ibid., 109.

[17]Ibid., 111.

[18]Ibid., 110.

[19]Ibid.

[20]Andrew Wheatcroft, *The Ottomans: Mirroring Images* (New York, Penguin Press, 1997), 67.

[21]Christian I.Archer, *World History of Warfare* (University of Nebraska Press, Lincoln, 2002), 227.

[22]Ibid.

[23]Ibid.

[24]Ibid., 231.

[25]Historian James Waterson points rather to the use of the field artillery at that and other Mamluk-Ottoman battles as the deciding factor. Waterson, *The Knights of Islam*, 270.

[26]Ibid., 270.

[27]Max Boot, War *Made New: Weapons, Warriors, and the Making of the Modern World* (Penguin Books, London, 2006), 22.

[28]Hanson, *Carnage and Culture*, 235. There is also a detailed description of the Battle of Lepanto in The *Atlantic Monthly* 1, no. 2 (December 1857).

[29]Ibid., 234.

[30]Ibid.

[31]Virginia H. Aksan, and Daniel Goffman, ed., *The Early and Modern Ottomans: Remapping the Empire* (Cambridge University Press, Cambridge, 2007), 106. Ghazis is a word used synonymously with yayas in the Turkish language and is used by Greene to describe land soldiers that become sailors.

[32]Ibid.

[33]Ibid., 109.

CHAPTER 5

CONCLUSION AND RECOMMENDATIONS

The armies of the Middle East and Persia ruled the region from the pre-Islam

period until the fall of the Ottoman Empire in 1918. This thesis examined the armies of

Islamic empiric and non-empiric states from the Parthian Persians to the Ottomans and

their success or failure with technology, concepts, and tactics from outside the empire.

This thesis has shown that Islamic armies possess an ability to assimilate technology,

concepts, and tactics from external sources, but refuse to assimilate the associated culture

of that technology. Instead, they choose to use it in a distinctly Islamic manner.

The Parthian and Sassanid Persians first conquered the lands of Persia using a

refinement of pre-existing technology. The Parthian use of a cavalry-based system of

archers and lancers and later a heavy cavalry-based army enabled the Parthians to move

rapidly on a battlefield dominated by Greek and later Roman infantry. The Sassanids

merged of the archer and lancer into an all-purpose heavy cavalry soldier enabling the

Sassanids to follow their barrage of arrows with a rapid and heavily armored charge. The

Parthian and Sassanid Persians capitalized on improvements in technology, concepts, and

tactics and dominated Persia for over six centuries.

Mohammed ibn Abdullah and his army of the faithful gave rise to the people of

the Middle East as conquerors. The Muslims of the ―Golden Age of Islam" used their

horse archers and later ships to assimilate the surrounding regions through conquest or

colonization. The use of guile as well as technology enabled the armies of Islam from the

Companions of the Prophet to the Mamluks to control the Persia, the Levant, and North

Africa for well over 700 years. The Mamluks were the only army able to stop the conquest of the Mongols.

The end of the Muslim era of supremacy came during the reign of the Ottomans (1517-1918). The failure of the Ottomans to adopt a professional army and the failure of the Ottomans to create and maintain a navy are the two main military reasons for the collapse of the Empire. This collapse was not catastrophic, rather a slow decline over a four-hundred year period after the first failure of the Ottomans to capture Vienna in 1529 and the death of Suleiman the Magnificent in 1566[1]. Before the Ottomans, the pre-Islamic societies of Persia transformed themselves into an army capable of consolidating the region into an empire. The Muslims that followed had risen from the Bedouins of the desert into one of the largest empires in history. During the period of the Ottoman Empire technology, concepts, and tactics existed that the empire could have used to defeat their Western enemies, but the Ottomans failed to grasp them and therefore could not keep pace with their rivals in the East and West.[2]

The Ottoman Navy was successful at the first and second battles of Lepanto. While the combined navies of Spain, the Holy See, and Venice defeated them at the third Battle of Lepanto, the West could not continue their pursuit of the Ottomans as they could not emplace the land bases to support their Navy. This lack of threat to the Ottomans enabled them to ignore the Western navies. While the Ottoman Navy atrophied over centuries, it was also not necessary in maintaining the empire. The Ottomans realized how expensive a professional navy was and chose to keep their navy small as the threat to the empire was low.

The Ottomans did not create a professional army because it was a huge financial drain on the empire. A professional army was expensive.[3] The Ottomans countered this by creating a relatively small, but extremely professional core for their army, the Janissaries. The remainder of the army served short tours and could not master the increasingly complex technology, concepts, and tactics of the modern battlefield. This lessened the requirements on the Sultan and enabled him to field an enormous army. This army could not perform on the modern battlefield because it could not maximize the weapon of the day--the musket. The Ottomans, for cultural reasons including their reasoning that the individual warrior risking his life for a place in paradise, could not mass in the same manner as the Europeans and thus lost the ability to defeat the Europeans. In order to remain peers with their enemies, the Ottomans needed to create an army of professionals that could drill and fight like the Europeans. This army could not be created because to do so would force the Sultan to become dependent on the people rather than the people remaining dependent on the Sultan. The Ottomans did not know how to use the technology, therefore, their units did not have the same firepower as the Europeans.

A professional army requires competent leadership. In the Ottoman Empire, leadership came from the Sultan and passed to his direct relatives. The mantle of leadership was granted based on loyalty not merit. The Ottoman army was led by a relative of the Sultan or the Sultan himself. This poor leadership extended from the Sultan to his generals and even to the tactical level as leadership was granted through loyalty not merit. While there were reforms after the destruction of the Janissaries, the amount of money allocated to the army was not sufficient to maintain an army and pensions for the officers. This led to the quality of officer that was replaced during World War I nearly wholesale with German generals. Ottoman leadership outside of the Janissaries lacked professional training and therefore the Ottomans were unable to capitalize on opportunities at a level of war greater than tactical. The great operational leader of the Ottoman Empire was simply not in existence or at best very rare. While the Janissaries were able to perform amazing feats of tactical brilliance, the Ottoman army was unable to translate that tactical brilliance into operational success.

This failure to grasp modern concepts continued into the modern Islamic army period. In the four Arab-Israeli wars and the two United States-Iraq wars, Islamic armies have shown a continued failure to produce the operational and tactical leadership, tactical soldier skills, and mastery of technology to defeat even a small Western army.[4] The poor operational and tactical leadership brought on by a continued use of a loyal servants and relatives plagued armies in the Arab world. The modern Islamic armies have much difficulty in coordinating combined arms at the operational level. The mainly untrained and un-skilled soldiers, while numerous, continue to populate armies unable to combat Western armies. While in many cases equipped with the same weapons and technology as their Western counterpart, the tactical unit and individual soldier were unable to capitalize on that technology due to unfamiliarity brought on by lack of training. This lack of training is a product of a conscripted army rather than a professional army. The technology that is being imported wholly into the Islamic armies is not made for the mental model of the Islamic army, but rather for the Western army.

In order for an Islamic army to modernize, the agent of change must realize that there are cultural limits to consider. First, the system in place in the modern Islamic armies has been in place for centuries. The conscripted army of Egypt is not much different in mentality from the Ottomans. To change the way an Islamic army fight into a Western manner is not possible given the current political and social system. Unless the political and social system that the national leader depends on for his power base changes, sweeping changes are impossible.

Inside of those limits, there are options for professionalization of Islamic armies. Take, for example, the Saudi Arabian National Guard and the modern army of the Kingdom of Jordan. Both countries had substandard armies. During the second half of the 20th century, both nations began creating a professional army core, using foreign advisors, and sending their officers and non-commissioned officers to foreign military education. As a result of these innovative steps, they have become modern, professional armies capable of conducting combined arms operations.

One option for an Islamic nation is the creation of a volunteer army. While expensive, the nation could create a smaller army that is highly trained rather than a large army that is poorly trained. A volunteer army creates loyalty to the nation and enables a nation to capitalize on soldiers who can achieve a higher training level than a two-year conscript based army can ever hope to achieve. While this option carries an amount of risk in the short term, over time, a nation that uses this option creates an army that can easily defeat a similar-sized conscript based army.

Using Western advisors to train an Islamic army provides a basic knowledge of Western tactics and technology. This infusion of knowledge assists the leadership of an army that may simply not know how to change itself from within. Western advisors are reasonably inexpensive to the host nation and can result in substantial change in a short amount of time.

Another option for a nation that wishes to modernize is educating their officer corps. By sending officers abroad on exchanges to more technologically mature nations, armies can populate their officer corps with those concepts unavailable in the home nation's military. Officers who attend another nation's military or civilian education opportunities bring back to the host nation and army another set of concepts that can spur further educational opportunities in the home nation's military.

In order for modern Islamic nations to bring their armies out of the Ottoman decay, they must professionalize. They must not just take the technology and use it within their cultural concepts. Islamic armies of the past possessed an ability to assimilate technology, concepts, and tactics from external sources, but refused to assimilate the associated culture of that technology. Instead, they chose to use it in a distinctly Islamic manner. They created massive land armies of untrained soldiers unable to capitalize on modern technology, concepts, and tactics

Large armies may appear to be strong, but it is only the professional army, large or small, that can defeat another professional army. The Jordanians and Saudis have realized this and have remodeled their armies into more professional ones able to fight in a combined arms manner. This may spur other nations to professionalize and lead to a reinvigoration of the Islamic army into something that may rival the ‑Golden Age of Islam."

---

[1]Several scholars including Phillip K. Hitti, Bernard Lewis, and Sir John Glubb regard 1566 as the beginning of the declination of the Ottoman Empire.

[2]Some, including classicist Victor Hanson, propose that the lack of competition within the Ottoman Empire, or more likely, the existence of much competition within the European states, led to the military arms race in pre-Modern Europe.

[3]The first example of a modern professional army is the Prussians. Their transformation from a conscript-based army begins the rise of the professional army in Europe.

[4]For examples of all of these wars, consult Kenneth M. Pollack, *Arabs at War: Military Effectiveness, 1948-1971* (Lincoln, NE: University of Nebraska Press, 2002).

BIBLIOGRAPHY

Aksan, Virginia H. *Ottoman Wars 1700-1870: An Empire Beseiged.* Harlow, UK: Pearson Education, Ltd., 2007.

Aksan, Virginia H., and Daniel Goffman, ed. *The Early Modern Ottomans: Remapping the Empire.* Cambridge: Cambridge University Press, 2007.

Al-Azmh, Aziz. *The Times of History: Universal Topics in Islamic Hstoriography.* Budapest: Central European Press, 2007.

Archer, Christian I., et al. *World History of Warfare.* Lincoln, NE: University of Nebraska Press, 2002.

Atkine, Norville de. "Why Arabs Lose Wars." *Middle East Review of International Affairs* (March 2000): 16-25.

Ayalon, David. *Gunpowder and Firearms in the Mamluk Kingdom: A Challenge to Mediaeval Society.* London: Frank Cass and Company, 1978.

Black, Jeremy. *Warfare in the Eighteenth Century.* London: Cassell, 1999.

Blankenship, Khalid Yahya. *The End of the Jihad State: The Reign of Hisham Ibn Abd al-Malik and the Collapse of the Ummayids.* Albany, NY: The State University of New York Press, 1994.

Boot, Max. *War Made New: Weapons, Warriors, and the Making of the Modern World.* New York: Gotham Publishers, 2006.

Curtis, Vesta Sarkosh and Sarah Stewart, ed. *The Age of the Parthians: The Idea of Iran.* Vol. 2. London: IB Taurus and Co, 2007.

Dentan, Robert C., ed. *The Idea of History in the Ancient Near east.* New Haven, CT: Yale University Press, 1955.

DiMarco, Louis A. *Warhorse: A History of the Military Horse and Rider.* Yardley, PA: Westholme Publishing, 2008.

Dodgeon, Michael H. and Samuel N.C. Lieu, ed. *The Roman Eastern Frontier and the Persian wars (AD 226-363): A Documentary History.* London: Routledge Press, 1994.

Donner, Fred McGraw. *The Early Islamic Conquests.* Princeton: Princeton University Press, 1981.

Edwell, Peter M. *Between Rome and Persia: The middle Euphrates, Mesopotamia, and Palmyra under Roman control.* London: Routledge Press, 2008.

Farrokh, Kaveh. *Shadows in the Desert: Ancient Persia at War.* Oxford: Osprey Publishing Ltd, 2007.

Finkel, Caroline. *Osman's Dream: the Story of the Ottoman Empire 1300-1923.* New York: Basic Books, 2005.

Frye, Richard N. *The Heritage of Persia.* Cleveland: The World Publishing Company, 1963.

Gabriel, Richard A, and Karen S. Metz, *A Short History of War: The Evolution of Warfare and Weapons.* Carlisle Barracks, PA: Strategic Studies Institute, 1992.

Glubb, Sir Phillip. *A Short History of the Arab Peoples.* New York: Stein and Day, 1969.

Goffman, Daniel. *The Ottoman Empire and Early Modern Europe.* Cambridge: Cambridge University Press, 2002.

Gordon, Matthew S. *The Rise of Islam.* Westport, CT: Greenwood Press, 2005.

Hanson, Victor Davis. *Carnage and Culture.* New York: Anchor Books, 2001.

Hawting, G.R. *The First Dynasty of Islam: The Ummayid Caliphate AD 661-750.* London: Routledge Press, 2000.

Hitti, Phillip K. *The Arabs: A Short History.* New York: St Martin's Press, 1968.

Hodgson, Marshall G.S. *The Venture of Islam: Conscience and History in a World Civilization.* Vol. 2: The Expansion of Islam in the Middle Periods. Chicago: The University of Chicago Press, 1974.

Hodgson, Mashall G.S. *The Venture of Islam: Conscience and History in a World Civilization.* Vol. 1: The Classical Age of Islam. Chicago: The University of Chicago Press, 1974.

Hogsdon, Marshall G.S. *The Venture of Islam: Conscience and History in a World Civilization.* Vol. 3: The Gunpowder Empire and Modern Times. Chicago: The University of Chicago Press, 1974.

Holt, P.M., Ann K.S. Lambton, and Bernard Lewis, . *The Cambridge History of Islam.* Vols. IA The Central Islamic Lands from the Pre-Islamic Times to the First World War. Cambridge: Cambridge University Press, 1979.

Karsh, Efriam. *Islamic Imperialism: A History.* Cambridge, MA: Yale University Press, 2007.

Kennedy, Hugh. *Great Arab Conquests: How the Spread of Islam Changed the World We Live in.* Philadelphia: Da Capo Press, 2007.

———. *When Baghdad Ruled the Muslim World: the Rise and Fall of Islam's Greatest Dynasty.* Cambridge, MA: Da Capo Press, 2004.

Lapidus, Ira M. *A History of Islamic Societies.* Cambridge: Cambridge University Press, 1988.

Lepper, F. A. *Trajan's Parthian War.* Chicago: Ares Publisher, Inc., 1993.

Lewis, Bernard, ed. *Islam and the Arab World: Faith, People, Culture.* New York: Alfred A. Knopf, Inc., 1976.

———. *The Middle East: A Brief History of the Last 2,000 Years.* New York: Scribener Press, 1995.

Nafzinger, George F., and Mark W. Walton, *Islam at War.* Weston, CT: Praegar, CT, 2003.

Olmstead, A. T. *History of the Persian Empire.* Chicago: The University of Chicago Press, 1948.

Panaite, Viorel. *The Ottoman Law of War and Peace: The Ottoman empire and Tribute Payers.* Boulder: East European Monographs, 2000.

Pollack, Kenneth M. *Arabs at War: Military Effectiveness, 1948-1991.* Lincoln, NE: University of Nebraska Press, 2002.

Rogerson, Barnaby. *The Heirs of Mohammed: Islam's First century and the Origins of the Sunni-Shia Split.* New York: The Overlook Press, 2006.

Rouse, W.H.D., trans. *The March up Country: A Translation of Xenophon's Anabasis.* Ann Arbor: The University of Michigan Press, 1964.

Siddiqi, Amir H. *Decisive Battles of Islam.* LAhore, Pakistan: Islamic Book Publishers, 1986.

Sidebottom, Harry. *Ancient Warfare: A Very Short Introduction.* New York: Oxford University Press, 2004.

Spaulding, Oliver Lyman and Nickerson, Hoffman. *Ancient and Medieval Warfare.* New York: Barnes and Noble Books, 1993.

Waterson, James. *The Knights of Islam: The Wars of the Mamluks.* London: Greenhill Books, 2007.

Wilcox, Peter. *Rome's Enemies (3): Parthians and Sassanid Persians.* London: Osprey Publishing Ltd, 1986.

www.ingramcontent.com/pod-product-compliance
Lightning Source LLC
Chambersburg PA
CBHW081850280526
45789CB00007B/2641